SEEKING SANCTUARY

SEEKING SANCTUARY

Journeys to Sudan

Hilda Reilly

Published by Eye Books

Edited by Chris Davison

Seeking Sanctuary
1st Edition
February 2005

Published by Eye Books Ltd
51 Boscombe Rd
London
W12 9HT
Tel/fax: +44 (0) 20 8743 3276
website: www.eye-books.com

Cover photographs by Tom Gething -
Author photograph by Claire Contentin

Set in Frutiger and Garamond
ISBN: 1903070392

British Library Cataloguing in Publication Data
A catalogue record for this book is available from the British Library

Printed and bound in Great Britain by Biddles Ltd

In memory of Babiker

the most endearing of Sudanese

Acknowledgements

This book has come about thanks to the support of all those who have contributed to its making. I would like to thank in particular Mikal Mahmoud and his wife Fatima, Mohammed Abdul Qaadir, Molly, Naimah and Zarina Davies who generously spent hours recounting their personal stories; Griselda El Tayib, Jane Anne, Lena Winfrey and Abdel Karim who shared with me their knowledge of Islam and Sudan as well as some of their own experiences; Professor Tigani Hassan of the Faith Research Centre in Khartoum who taught me much about Islamic beliefs and practices. Rianne Tamis and Maha El Amin helped out as interpreters when my own Arabic wasn't up to the task and Shane Abdel Nour provided invaluable comments and corrections after reading the first draft of the manuscript. Nagla and Mustapha made 'their house my house' in typical Sudanese fashion; Selma, Somaya and Amal made my visit to Zariba such fun; Abdel Rahman Karroug was a constant source of common sense and practical advice. Thanks are also due to Vicki, Yin and Mai for their support and hospitality during my last visit to Sudan, and to la famille Contentin – Guy, Chantal and Claire – who helped me to finish the book by providing a tres chalereux roof over my head when my Italian Place in the Sun turned into the Holiday Home from Hell. Finally to Tom Gething for allowing his photographs to be used for the cover.

To all – shoukran.

Contents

1 INTRODUCTION

A Place in the Sun, No Going Back, Living the Dream, Costa Living, Get a New Life....In recent years British television schedules have been awash with programmes documenting the experiences of people who have upped sticks and gone to settle abroad. Tired of the rat race, seeking to give more meaning to their lives, or simply wanting change, they leave their jobs, sell up and head off south to reinvent themselves as farmers, shopkeepers, hoteliers – free spirits of whatever kind – in places as diverse as Andalucia and Zambia, Tasmania and Tuscany.

Sudan at the beginning of the 21st century was not a country you would expect to find on this list: one of the poorest countries in the world, governed by a hardline fundamentalist Islamic government, riven by a longstanding civil war, and considered a hardship posting for expats. Yet it had become one of the hotspots for Muslim converts from the West who felt that they could fully live their newly adopted Islamic life only by moving to an Islamic environment.

Mikal, Zarina, Mohammed, Naimah and Molly – two British and three American – have all left their home countries and are now living in Sudan. In this book they tell the story of their twin journeys from their previous religion to Islam, and from their culture of origin to that of their adopted country. Their personal stories are rounded out with contributions from other sources, both foreign converts and Sudanese Muslims.

My interest in these stories began when I was myself living in Sudan, between 1999 and 2004. It was a time when Islam was increasingly becoming a mainstay of the headline writers.

Osama Bin Laden had already attracted attention with his alleged involvement in the bombing of the American embassies in Nairobi and Dar es Salaam, followed by the retaliatory American bombing of the Shifa pharmaceutical factory in Khartoum where he purportedly financed the production of chemical weapons. Three years later the media focus on Islam intensified with the Twin Tower attacks. The belief that Muslim was a synonym for terrorist gained more ground while stories such as those of Richard Reid, the shoe–bomber, John Walker Lindh, the young Californian who fought with the Taliban, and Frenchman Jerome Courtailler, charged with involvement in a plan to bomb the US embassy in Paris – to name but a few – gave conversion a bad name.

In the course of my work in Sudan I came across several Western converts who had opted for long–term residence in the country. The first of these was Khalid, an African–American in his late 30s who had been living in Sudan for about ten years when I met him. At the time, I was running an educational charity in Khartoum and was always on the lookout for people to teach in the language school that I had set up as an income generator. Khalid came into my office one day, looking for work. Clad in traditional Sudanese dress – white *jellabiya* and white turban – he had the good looks and easy charm of a Tiger Woods.

Khalid wasn't a teacher but that was not an obstacle. As in so many other countries where people are avid to learn English, the Sudanese students' first priority was to be taught from the mouth of a native English speaker. Khalid was keen, pleasant and eager to do a good job. I gave him a thrice–weekly class of elementary students.

After his first lesson one of the other teachers, a young British man, came to me aghast. "You can't give that class to Khalid. The students won't have it. They won't come any more."

"Why ever not?"

"He's an *Ansar al Sunna*. The students don't like people with these extreme views."

The *Ansar al Sunna* – Followers of Tradition – is a strict

Islamic sect whose adherents base their lifestyle on that of the Prophet Mohammed. They wear distinctive short *jellabiyas* and long beards, and are not all that popular with the average, more moderate Sudanese. Khalid's *jellabiya* was not particularly short but the fact that, as a foreigner, he wore one at all, coupled with his beard, marked him out as someone with strong religious views. However, the mass defection predicted by Vince did not come about and the students rejoiced in his American accent and his friendly manner.

Khalid's lifestyle seemed like a Sudanese version of *The Good Life*. He lived in an outlying area of Khartoum in a traditional mud–brick house with the rooms grouped round a courtyard. His two wives, one Sudanese and one American, lived in separate parts of the compound with their respective children. There were seven children altogether and it was difficult to see how Khalid managed to support the two families. Originally a photographer back in Louisiana, he had experimented with different money–making activities in Sudan. Good with his hands, he set himself up as a shoemaker and got by until he lost his tools. Back in the US for a visit he bought some new cobbling equipment but discovered at the airport check–in that his luggage was over the weight limit. Hey, he said to a baggage handler, would you just look out for this box while I try and sort things out, and off he went to organise a redistribution of bags among the people he was travelling with. When he came back the box had been removed by the police. So he turned to tailoring and made a modest living until his sewing machine broke down. After working for me for some months he saved up enough money to set up his next enterprise. This was a hardware shop, a little retail outlet which he ran from his home compound, selling light bulbs, washers, nuts and bolts, plugs, cables, lengths of pipe. He radiated enthusiasm as he talked of his plans. This was what he really wanted to do – run his own little business serving the local community. But after a few months he was back again with his tail between his legs. It hadn't worked out.

But they survived. Khalid had not only adapted to the spartan lifestyle, he embraced it eagerly. Now and again he hired a pickup truck and went to the market where he bought vast quantities of everything they needed at bulk prices. The family diet was supplemented by eggs and milk from the hens and goats for which Khalid was forever fixing up runs and pens. And there was the teaching work that he did for me intermittently.

Some time later Khalid acquired a third wife, a young girl who lived in a country village. Khalid liked to get out of Khartoum and go roaming around the countryside. During his travels he had got to know a family of simple people with whom he felt greatly at ease. He visited them often and after a while asked for the hand of one of the daughters. The girl stayed on in the village after the marriage, with Khalid joining her at weekends. He described with an innocent excitement the extra room that the family had built for them in their compound, the four mud–brick walls set in an oasis of fresh air and tranquillity. A few months later he announced that they were all – the first two wives and the seven children – going down to live in the Gezira.

He turned up in Khartoum from time to time after that with very upbeat accounts of their experiences. He loved the new life in the country, the wives were content and the kids were having a whale of a time. The only negative report was of a snake bite which had hospitalised him for two days. While chopping wood with some other men he had noticed that his brother–in–law wasn't wearing shoes and gave him his – whereupon a snake shot its head out of the woodpile and bit his foot.

That was Khalid. "Hey, you're not wearing shoes? Here, take mine."

In March 2004 there was a tremendous press furore as five British detainees in Guantánamo Bay were released and flown back to Britain. "Arrest these traitors the minute they set foot on British soil." screeched the Sun, while other papers had a field day with epithets such as "Tipton Taliban", "Taliban tourists", "terror tourists".

Nothing could more clearly highlight the equivalence in people's minds: Muslim = terrorist.

One of the five, Ronald Fiddler from Manchester – who changed his name to Jamal al–Harith when he converted to Islam – was released the minute the plane landed as there appeared to be no grounds at all for holding him for further questioning. Reports indicated that since converting Jamal had had a keen interest in visiting Muslim countries; he had even spent four years in Khartoum in the 1990s, learning Arabic and teaching English. According to Jamal, he had been hitch–hiking in Pakistan in September 2001 when the lorry he was travelling in was stopped by some Taliban soldiers who arrested him when they saw that he had a British passport. He spent the next few months in Kandahar jail where the Americans found him – sharing the space with a donkey which had been arrested because its owner had been using it for the transport of stolen goods. Just as the Red Cross were arranging to fly him to the British consulate in Kabul the CIA whisked him off to Guantánamo Bay. Another Guantánamo detainee, Moazzam Begg from Birmingham, had gone to Afghanistan with his wife and three children in 2001 to work on a literacy project. After 9/11 he took his family to Pakistan for safety and was arrested there in February 2002. Yet another, Asif Iqbal from Tipton, had gone to Pakistan to meet the bride his family had found for him.

I thought how easily, especially if Bin Laden had still been in Sudan, some of the Western converts might have ended up in Guantánamo Bay. "Are we seriously expected to believe they were there enjoying the weather and the views?" the Sun asked, enquiring about the reasons for the detainees being in Afghanistan. Would those who have only preconceived and negative notions about Sudan seriously believe that people had gone there of their own free will because they preferred it to life in the West? What would the Sun have made of Khalid bumbling around an American airport, with thick long beard and Islamic dress, trying to get someone to take charge of a box of shoemaking equipment for him?

But the press must have a good story. I was reminded of reporting in the British press in 1999 when a state of emergency was declared in Sudan. Life carried on just as usual. In fact, the first I heard of it was through the BBC World Service. Yet on going to the Internet for more information I found articles by journalists making wild claims about what was going on. Sudan was "on the brink of fighting that would make Beirut seem a picnic," wrote one. Another described the atmosphere in Khartoum as "eerily quiet". It may have seemed eerie to him that a capital city should be so sober but that was just the way it always was.

Yazin, the husband of a British convert, told me about a foreign visitor he had met in Khartoum. He had been warned that Sudan was much more dangerous than Kenya and that he mustn't go out at night or mix with the locals. He came to the country expecting to find 'something like barbarians'.

"But he decided to be a little adventurous so he mixed within the Sudanese community to find that all the ideas he came with were all wrong. He couldn't believe that people sleep outside in the open air with not a very secure outside wall and he was astonished. And the way kids play outside and they're really safe. He was even more amazed when he went visiting villages outside Khartoum, the way that people who don't know him wanted to show him their generosity, the way everybody insisted that he goes to the house, just maybe to drink a glass of water."

My dentist had similar erroneous ideas.

"You don't *look* like a Rambo," he said, peering at me over the top of his face mask, when I told him that I had spent the last five years in Sudan. I pointed to a couple of crowns that I'd had done in Khartoum. He prodded them with his probe. "Hmm, not bad, not bad at all. I thought all they could do was shoot Kalashnikovs."

Our ideas are often based on groundless assumptions.

After talking with my first interviewee it occurred to me that my line of questioning had been similar to which one might adopt when talking with a delinquent to discover the flaws in his character, the deficiencies of his upbringing, that led to his life of crime. Why do we assume that people converting to Islam must be running away from something, or that this radical change in their lives can only have been catalysed by some personal trauma?

An early email from my editor referred to 'the sacrifices these people have made to dedicate their lives to Islam in a challenging environment like Sudan'. But they don't think of it as sacrifice, or at the very least they would say that the negative aspects of life in Sudan are less than the negative aspects of life in America or Europe; also that they are outweighed by the positive aspects of life in Sudan.

There seems to be a notion that being a Muslim is a bit like being a monk or a nun, that they are depriving themselves of enjoyment and adopting a harsh lifestyle as a trade–off for the prospect of rewards in the hereafter. They don't drink, the women wear uncomfortable clothes, they marry people they have never met before and so on. But for people who make the choice and convert to Islam of their own free will these things are clearly not problems.

Alcohol is such an integral part of social life in the West that we can't imagine being without it. To me, coming from a Scottish drinking culture, a social event without alcohol is like a meal without salt. Yet one tenth of the world's population chew betel nut, a sizeable number chew qat, and it never crosses our minds to feel deprived because we don't use these stimulants.

Muslims are not the only people to have dress codes forced on them. Western fashion can also be dictatorial in coercing women into looking ridiculous or feeling uncomfortable. The stiletto–heeled winkle–pickers of the 1960s were like instruments of torture but we wouldn't have set foot outside the door without them. The 'fifties revisited' styles of winter 2003 embellished nobody but people wore them rather than be thought not up to date.

Muslims are often criticised for some of their beliefs and practices. But is this because we assume that what is the norm for us is necessarily right? Is being a co–wife, for example, any more emotionally difficult than having siblings? If a society imposed the one–child family as the norm, if this was enforced by law, it would become the standard situation in that society. The children would look askance at other societies where more children were allowed and wonder how those children could cope with not having their mother and father all to themselves, not being the sole object of their love and attention. They would find it difficult to believe that the parents could love all their children equally.

My contact with Khalid and other converts heightened my awareness of an imbalance in the perception and reporting of Islam and its adherents. No news is good news, as the saying goes, and conversely good news is no news. We hear about Richard Reid, John Walker Lindh and Jerome Courtailler but not about the many Muslim converts who are quietly going about their business and bothering nobody. We hear about Muslim converts being snatched up by the CIA in Arab countries, often in exchange for a payment to the locals who hand them over, and play up the terrorism angle – because it makes a better news story. Likewise with Sudan we know about the war, the harsh government, the intolerable climate, but little about the culture and lifestyle of what must be one of the friendliest and most easy–going peoples in the world. My hope is that the converts' stories about their Sudanese experiences will help to redress the balance both for Islam and for Sudan.

2 MAKING ACQUAINTANCE

I had been living in Khartoum for more than four years when I started talking with the converts. I already knew Mikal Mahmoud, Mohammed Abdul Qaadir and Khalid very well as they all worked for me as teachers. Mikal and Khalid, in particular, had been with me for most of my time in Sudan and were unfailingly supportive to me in what were at times very difficult situations. They were also tremendous fun to be with. I could get a different perspective on even the direst problems when I viewed them through the prism of their sense of humour. Mikal's great hearty guffaws and his down–to–earth cynicism would always lift my spirits, and Khalid's gentler whimsy was cosily reassuring. Mohammed came later and worked for me for about three months. He was a much younger man – in his late 20s whereas Khalid was about 40 and Mikal about ten years older – so I didn't develop quite the same camaraderie with him as I did with the other two who were nearer my own age. All three were African–American.

I knew of a number of other Western converts living in Sudan. I started tracking them down in the hope that they would be willing to tell their stories. Many of them were not.

I had heard of a Dutch man working at Shendi University, about 100 miles north of Khartoum, who had been a Muslim for a number of years and had recently married a woman of the Ja'alin tribe. I managed to get through to him on the phone at the university. He responded enthusiastically to my proposal and fixed a time for me to phone again the next day so that we could arrange to meet either in Shendi or Khartoum. When I called back he wasn't there. The woman who answered said he had left a message to say that he had changed his mind. He had given no reason.

The PR man at a mosque in Khartoum gave me the phone number of a British woman who had been living in Sudan for twenty–five years. She had married a Sudanese man after converting to Islam and joining one of the Sudanese Sufi sects. I called her. She seemed keen on the idea but said that she would have to ask her husband before she could agree to take part. He had just left the country for a six–week visit to Europe. When I phoned back a couple of months later she refused, saying that she had once agreed to be interviewed by a journalist who had gone on to misrepresent her in his article and she didn't want to risk a repeat experience.

An Italian convert who belonged to the same sect was unexpectedly hospitalised on the day we were supposed to meet. She then left the country.

I wrote to the manager of an international courier company in Khartoum, a British convert who had previously spoken to me most eloquently about his conversion and life in Sudan. He responded by fixing a meeting, but later cancelled it and then put the shutters up.

Two left Sudan before I had a chance to catch up with them. They were female American converts who had just moved to Sudan with their children to work at BEI, a private English–medium school. They had been unable to settle in. Life in Sudan, particularly in the school environment where the children were from well–off families and often quite Westernised, was insufficiently Islamic for them. They had expected a much stricter environment with separation of the sexes at social gatherings, strict observance of the Islamic dress code, meals taken sitting on the floor, eating with the hands and so on. Not finding it they quickly went back to east coast America where there are now social enclaves and educational establishments which correspond more closely to the conditions they were seeking.

Khalid, after initially agreeing, withdrew after pressure from friends who suggested that there might be something sinister in what I was doing. In the existing political climate this was understandable. Others simply felt that it was a private matter that they didn't want to discuss with a stranger.

Mikal had told me about the African University, a private university on the outskirts of Khartoum which runs subsidised programmes, funded by wealthy philanthropists from the Gulf, for foreign Muslims wishing to study Arabic and Islamic subjects. I thought it might be a good place to find more converts and so I asked my friend Angelo, a Southern Christian who was studying Arabic there, to make some enquiries for me. He called me the next day to tell me that he had spoken to Ustaz Mohammed Osman, a lecturer in charge of the foreigners. I phoned Ustaz Mohammed.

"Ah, I am very pleased you have called. I have been trying to phone you. All day I have been trying to phone. I want to speak to you. I have two Americans here, they are converts, I want you to meet them. Can you come on Saturday morning, please, 8.30. It will be very interesting for you?"

On the Saturday I picked my way through the sand– and rubble–strewn streets of downtown Khartoum, heading for the bus station in Souk Arabi to get a bus to the university.

Around the market, street vendors sitting behind sheets of sacking and flattened cardboard boxes sold every small item under the sun, as if lorryloads of goods from Poundland stores had been upended and scattered among them. Beggars with leprous stumps or the shrivelled limbs of polio reached out to me. Diners sat on plastic chairs at metal tables, eating from metal bowls in white–tiled cafeterias with the chill ambience of a public toilet. Fruit juice stalls did brisk trade as people sought to slake their thirst with mango, grapefruit, orange, guava. Shoeshine boys ran around in groups of twos and threes, rattling castanets made of shoe polish tins to announce their presence. Tailors pedalled the treadles of ancient sewing machines. Customers at a street barber sat on paint tins and bits of demolished building, watching the barber's hands at work on shards of broken mirror stuck to the wall in front of them. A cacophony of Arab music roared from the open–fronted retailing booths, each one trying to drown out the sounds of his neighbour.

Rows of buses lined up, waiting to set off as soon as the seats were filled. Fare collectors hung out from the doorways in acrobatic pose, rattling coins in their hands and calling the names of their destination. "Burri, Burri, Burri," shouted one. "Soba Aradi, Soba Aradi, Soba Aradi," bawled the next. I got into one heading for Erkoweit.

Half an hour later I arrived at the African University, a well–appointed place in pleasantly landscaped grounds dotted with white–trunked king palms. I made my way to Ustaz Mohammed's office. He wasn't there but emerged briefly from a lecture theatre to delegate someone else to take me to another office for the meeting.

"Go with Ahmed, please. They are waiting for you."

"These men are converts but they are not Americans," Ahmed said as we walked along. "They are from an Arab country."

This wasn't what I was after but as I was already there I thought I might as well speak to them. In any case, they might know other students with the profile I wanted.

Ahmed introduced me to the man in whose office I was to wait and left me saying, "Just wait. I don't know how long."

Half an hour passed while a stream of people came and went on some administrative business. Most of them were men. The few women were heavily clad in full Islamic dress. I finally asked the man behind the desk where the people I was waiting for were.

"They're not here. Come back tomorrow."

"But I was told to come today."

"Well, they're not here. Come tomorrow."

"But Ustaz Mohammed...."

"They're not here. Tomorrow." He spoke in a tone that brooked no argument and resumed his paperwork.

I thought about something that Mohammed Abdul Qaadir had

said when talking about one of his spiritual teachers:

"The sheikh there told us that to survive in Sudan you need five things. He said the first thing is patience, the second thing is also patience, and the third thing is patience, and the fourth thing is patience again, and then he said the fifth thing is also patience. And so he said you must be patient until patience itself becomes patient. He spoke in relation to Sudan specifically but it applies to life in general. One of the greatest tests in life is that one must have patience."

Patience paid off in the end. I heard that Naimah, an American convert whom I knew by repute, was back in the country. She had come to settle in Sudan in 1998 with her own personal agenda of humanitarian work that she wanted to carry out but had left to take a job in China for a couple of years. Then I was put in touch with Molly who had married a Sudanese and had subsequently become a devout Muslim. And I came across Zarina again, a British woman I had met a few years previously but who had disappeared from sight. All three were keen to talk about their relationship with Islam and their lives in Sudan.

Several others talked about specific aspects of Islam and Sudan.

Griselda El Tayib, wife of the renowned Arabic scholar, Professor Abdulla El Tayib, came to Sudan in the late 1940s and has accumulated a fund of piquant stories and trenchant views in the years since. One of the first relates to her sea voyage out from England after she got married. She was travelling without her husband and shared a cabin with three other British women. She mentioned to them that she was married to a Sudanese. "Well, I think that's absolutely disgusting," said one of the women – and refused to speak to her for the rest of the voyage.

Jane Anne taught me to ride. She and her husband Yazin have a farm and a riding school in Khartoum, populated mostly by horses which they have rescued from a variety of sorry Sudanese conditions. As I ambled round the paddock on Black Beauty or trotted back and forth between poles, picking socks out of cans,

Jane Anne would keep up a flow of stories and pithy comments, punctuated by the occasional brisk instruction about my hands or my back or the reins or the angle of my feet in the stirrups. She pulls no punches when it comes to saying what she thinks.

Lena Winfrey, an American woman, was living in Sudan with her Jordanian husband whom she had married after converting to Islam in the United States. She is writing a book about Islam for non–Muslims.

Abdel Karim, a British convert who had been living in Sudan for some years, expressed his views on issues he felt strongly about but preferred not to talk about his personal life.

Between them, they have put together a foreigner's eye view of life in the Islamic north of Sudan as well as charting their individual courses in getting there.

3 SKETCHING OUT SUDAN

When I first went to Khartoum in February 1999 a recent article in the *London Evening Standard* had included Sudan in its black–list of countries not to be visited on any account. The *Lonely Planet* travel guide was equally discouraging, with grim warnings about war and bandits. Even the British Ambassador had felt obliged to say to me (albeit tongue–in–cheek), "It is, of course, my duty as a member of the Foreign Office to advise you that you shouldn't go to Sudan."

Working as the director of a Sudanese charity I was not cocooned in the privileged lifestyle of typical expats such as embassy staff, oil company employees or even people working with international NGOs. In the early days particularly I had little in the way of either comfort or entertainment. I had no satellite television and no radio apart from an hour or so of interference–ridden BBC World Service in the morning. The only English newspapers available – at the British Council – were two or three weeks out of date. Internet access was expensive and fraught with technical difficulties. There were no cultural activities, few restaurants and of course no alcohol. The once–thriving Jamhurriya Street – the 'Champs Elysees' of Khartoum in the fifties and sixties – was now run–down and semi–deserted. The average grocery shop was an open–fronted booth with a limited range of goods: vats of white cheese; packets of tasteless biscuits; tinned fish; jars of poor–quality jam; baskets of rice and pulses; oil and soap powder ladled out into little plastic bags; candles, matches, milk and yoghurt; that was about it. For the better–off and foreigners a number of mini–marts with imported products were beginning to appear but they were expensive. The harsh climate restricted the types of vegetable available which meant that my usual vegetarian diet was curtailed. On top of that there was the intolerable heat, made even more unbearable by the power cuts that became increasingly frequent and prolonged as summer advanced. The tumbledown house I lived in had a leaking roof, and plumbing and electrical installations which would have defied Bob the Builder. In my bleaker moments it seemed that not much had changed since G.W. Steevens, author of *With Kitchener to Khartoum*, had described Sudan as 'a God-accursed wilderness, an empty limbo of torment for ever and ever'. How people could choose to come from the West to settle permanently in Sudan, some of them in conditions much more austere than mine, was beyond me at that time.

Jane Anne, who had married Yazin in England in the 1980s, lasted only six weeks when she first arrived in 1988.

"When I came it was in the middle of the rainy season and a couple of the houses fell down across the road from us, the electricity cut off and we didn't have any electricity for about a week. I was living in this house here and although we had a generator there was a problem with the diesel so we could only have the generator on a certain amount of time during the day. It was boiling hot and I wasn't used to the heat anyway and there were mosquitoes everywhere because there were puddles of water outside because the water doesn't drain properly and you know *(peals of laughter...)* I thought, I just can't cope with this. I got malaria, my daughter Aisha got malaria and she was just two and a half. Everyone was getting malaria and it was just awful. I didn't go anywhere because I didn't know anyone. You couldn't go anywhere anyway because there were puddles all over the place and it was muddy. And I just thought, that is it, I can't live here, and I left."

Two years later Jane Anne girded her loins and came back again.

"I decided before I came back that I had to put up with these things. It wasn't difficult. You *can* put up with things. You know, a lot of people can't. A lot of people would come here and say, oh the flies and the dust and you can't get what you want. I know it's a bit of a silly thing to say, Hilda, but you could never get a decent bar of chocolate. Even if you went to the Hilton it had been there such a long time it had little white spots on it and everything."

Communication was another problem. The Internet revolution had still not reached Sudan and even the telephone system was pretty basic.

"Oh, that was terrible, absolutely terrible," says Jane Anne. "You couldn't get through to England for weeks on end. Even in Sudan you couldn't get through. Half the day you couldn't get through from here to Omdurman. I didn't phone for about two months and the letters were pathetic as well. It was no good sending letters so my mum phoned up the British Embassy and the British Embassy said: Do you not realise that Sudan is at war? I mean, did that make my mum feel any better? I mean, the war's hundreds of miles away, but they said: Do you not realise Sudan's at war? And it was only through somebody knowing somebody that worked at the Embassy that they said your mum's phoned up the Embassy worried about you. I found somebody who had a phone that I could get through on and I phoned up and I said there's no problem, don't worry about it."

Jane Anne's inherent doughtiness enabled her to survive this time.

"I decided that I had to put up with it. If we didn't have electricity, I just wouldn't moan about it. I'd just get on with things, ignoring the heat. If we didn't have water then I would sort out that I had barrels filled with water so it wouldn't matter if there was water coming through the tap or not. I made up my mind about this before I came; otherwise I wouldn't have come back because it is very difficult living here."

The dire conditions which had daunted both Jane Anne and myself – the crumbling infrastructure, the lack of systems in place to cope with environmental difficulties, the dearth of consumer goods, the barren cultural and entertainment scene – were due largely to political and security factors. For most of the more than forty years since it had gained independence from the British in 1956 Sudan had been at war. Conflict had been and was still raging between the Muslim, Arabised North and the Christian/Animist African South, with disastrous effects on what had previously been a country with a healthy economy, a well–educated workforce and a strong potential for agricultural development.

The differences in socio–economic development between North and South had led, in 1963, to a rebellion by the Southerners who felt that the external colonialism of the British had been replaced by an internal colonialism by their Northern neighbours. Although the ensuing conflict had come to a halt in 1972 it broke out again after President Nimeiri introduced *sharia* law in 1983, a move which Southerners resented greatly as having nothing to do with them, and declared his intention to transform Sudan into a Muslim Arab state. The discovery and exploitation of vast oil reserves lying towards the south fanned the flames of the civil war as the Southerners believed that the oil revenues due to them were being hived off by the national government for the purchase of military machinery to be used against them.

The trend towards religious fundamentalism found elsewhere in the Middle East had started to catch on in Sudan in the mid–60s, with the Muslim Brotherhood, an extremist Islamist group, gathering support particularly among the student population.

In 1965 Hassan al Turabi, a charismatic figure who was later to be a key player in Sudanese politics, became leader of the Islamic Charter Front, a political party which aligned itself with the Muslim Brotherhood and was later renamed the National Islamic Front (NIF). He went on to mastermind the political and ideological development of the Islamic movement in Sudan.

Although fundamentalism was not popular with most Sudanese, both the NIF and the Muslim Brotherhood achieved singular success in recruiting from sections of middle–class youth and professionals. It was his increasing reliance on these groups for support that had led Nimeiri to implement *sharia* law, the system of Islamic legal codes which apply to all areas of human behaviour – civil, criminal, moral, personal. Overnight the character of nightlife in Khartoum changed as all the bottles of alcohol in the capital were rounded up by government forces and poured melodramatically into the Nile. Just as dramatic was the first public amputation at Kober prison attended by the judge who had ordered it. As the hand was sliced from the arm the judge, a sensitive man who was only doing what his job required of him, fainted. Public floggings were common and women in particular found their personal freedoms severely restricted.

The overthrow of Nimeiri in 1985 was followed by a period of instability and uncertainty under the premiership of Sadiq Al Mahdi, leader of the conservative Umma party and great–grandson of Mohammed Ibn Abdalla – the Mahdi – who defeated General Gordon and threw the British out of Sudan in 1885. This was brought to an end by the second coup of the decade in 1989 when a military government, the Revolutionary Command Council for National Salvation, was set up under General Omer Bashir. The imposition of *sharia* was reinforced, and political repression became fiercer. Sudan became increasingly isolated from its Arab neighbours and the economic situation deteriorated as money haemorrhaged away into the escalating conflict with the South. Blacklisted by the US as a sponsor of international terrorism, Sudan had played host to Osama Bin Laden, Carlos the Jackal, Abu Nidal and other terrorist leaders in the 90s. During his time there the super–wealthy Bin Laden had been actively engaged in helping to improve the country's infrastructure, building roads and bridges and endearing himself to the Sudanese in the process.

But despite the Islamic government and the lifestyle it imposed, it was not immediately clear why converts should be attracted to the religious environment of Sudan. The presence of a large non–Muslim population diluted the Islamic effect. The previously

Muslim North now had a large admixture of Southerners, with about two million displaced people living in camps around Khartoum alone. There was also the possibility that if and when the civil war came to an end concessions to non–Muslim lifestyles would have to be made to accommodate the wishes of the Southerners. It was unlikely that Islamic rules would continue to be uniformly enforced in a reunited Sudan or in Khartoum as the national capital. And beneath the laid–back surface layer of life there were political and social undercurrents that would surely perturb anyone who dug down to look.

Other features of life in Sudan, especially as I got to know it better, made it easier to understand the appeal of the country. In many of the world's poorer countries foreigners often comment on how nice the people are. In fact, it sometimes seems that the niceness of a population is directly proportional to its poverty level or to the degree of political repression practised there. Nowhere can this be more true than in Sudan. Ask any Sudanese what he likes about his country, his town, his village, and he will most likely say the people, the close–knit nature of the community, the neighbourliness.

My own closest neighbours were Ederdeary and Tahani. They lived across the road from me in a bleak house with peeling paint, furnished mainly with *angaraibs*, both inside and scattered around the *hosh*. Ederdeary, a man in his mid–40s, had a rough and ready scruffy look about him which did not seem to fit with his job as a public relations officer with a bank. He was assiduous about his devotions, trooping back and forward to the mosque for the five daily sets of prayer. His hobby was buying and selling cars at the Friday auction and most weeks the old banger which had appeared outside his house the previous Friday would be replaced by another old banger. Tahani, a gentle, astute woman, was about ten years younger than her husband. They had three children, all girls, and judging by the affection Ederdeary lavished on them he had none of the regrets we often expect from Muslim men about not having a son. It was relaxing to sit around with them, lying on the *angaraibs*, doing nothing in particular, glancing at the television, playing with the children and being plied with sugary *karkade* or mint tea. Sometimes I sat with Tahani in the kitchen while she had her *dukhan*, a Sudanese method of embellishing the skin by crouching naked under an all–enveloping cloak above a heap of burning coals mixed with sandalwood placed in a hole in the floor. Other family members lived there off and on: Hanadi, Ederdeary's sister who worked in a telephone exchange; his mother, who was slowly dying of cancer; Ahmed, an electrician, who would saunter over to my house whenever I had an electrical problem. Sometimes he could fix it, sometimes not. Next door to them was a Security building. The Security people were hated and feared by the Sudanese. Agents of a repressive regime, they pounced on anyone suspected of deviating from the hardline norm, often for the most trivial or capricious of reasons, and subjected them to punishing treatment in their premises or in the many 'ghost houses' scattered across Khartoum. The family seemed unperturbed by the proximity of their notorious neighbours.

Round the corner lived a Sudanese–German family. Angela, the wife, had converted to Islam years after she married. Like all the other foreigners I knew who had converted after marrying a Sudanese Muslim she emphasised that there had been no pressure on her from the family. On the contrary, they had encouraged her in the practice of her previous religion (Catholicism), even driving her to church on Sundays. Then one day, while driving across Omdurman Bridge, she had a mystical experience which convinced her that Islam was the one true religion. She returned home immediately to tell her husband and sons who all cried with joy. She straight away said the *shahada*.

Angela and her husband were *Ansar al Sunna* types and the only people I met in Sudan who tried to encourage me to convert to Islam. Angela invited me round a couple of times for tea and home–made German *kuche*. The talk was all about Islam and finished with her pressing on me some proselytising literature. A few weeks later I phoned her. Her husband answered. He had been in bed for ten days with a slipped disc, he told me, and welcomed the enforced idleness as it gave him so much time to read the Koran. He had also been using the time to pray for me, he added, and asked if I'd read the books Angela gave me. I would remain in his prayers, he said, in the hope that I would soon be led to Islam.

Angela, a tall, imposing Valkyrie–like woman in her fifties, wore the *hijab* and maintained strict observance of Islamic behavioural rules. She would never, for example, allow herself to be in a room alone with a man. It could result in improper behaviour occurring, she explained, though this seemed hardly likely in view of her age and her air of inflexible rectitude. Her husband was similarly observant. Seeing him approaching me one day in the street I switched my bag from the right hand to the left in readiness to shake hands with him. "I don't shake hands with women," he called out at once, and pressed his hand to his chest in the alternative greeting used by those who refuse all physical contact with women. Their two handsome, well–brought up sons were every mother's dream: helpful, friendly and courteous, and with no scruples about handshaking.

In contrast, my neighbours at the other side were a couple of *bon vivants* who had no time for religion and let neither *sharia* law nor the nearness of the Security people stand in the way of their having a good time. Abdel Gadir was a Sudanese who had lived abroad for a long time, a 50–year–old going on 15, a doctor who moonlighted as a disc jockey. He had an impressive set of disco equipment which he sometimes used for parties in his own garden. On these nights the ghetto blasting sounds of the latest pop music could be heard from half a kilometre away. Curiously enough, the authorities didn't object to this kind of thing as long as it didn't continue beyond eleven o'clock. And as Jamila, his wife, told me, they always sent a hamper of goodies round to the people in the Security building beforehand to make sure that they didn't come to take a closer look at what they were doing.

What they were doing often involved alcohol which, despite *sharia* law, was always readily available in Sudan. You had the choice of the locally produced aragi, a date–based spirit with an unpleasant whiff of benzene about it, or black–market products at vastly inflated prices.

Invited to one of their parties one night, I turned up fairly late, having gone first to another function. As I went in I had the feeling that something was amiss. There was no music and very little talking. The guests were sitting round staring at Abdel Gadir who stood in the middle of the room facing a burly uncouth–looking man in a dirty *jellabiya*, rather in the manner of wrestlers just about to get to grips with one another.

The uncouth man had a sheet of A4 paper rolled up into a cone shape. He raised it to Abdel Gadir's mouth, told him to breathe into it and then stuck his own nose into the coneful of Abdel Gadir's breath. One by one all the guests were put through the same Heath Robinson–like procedure and then taken away to a van. I began to feel nervous that my own gin–scented breath would be subjected to examination and glanced worriedly at the uncouth–looking man. He waved his hand dismissively and gave me a conspiratorial leer to indicate that I, as a foreigner, was exempt.

Jamila told me later what had happened. Of the ten or so people arrested, she had been found guilty under Act 78 of introducing alcohol into the house, Abdel Gadir had been found guilty under Act 79 of receiving alcohol into the house and a third person had been found guilty of being drunk. They were all sentenced to be flogged but were told that the flogging would not be carried out if they could prove that they were diabetic. As Abdel Gadir was a doctor, the 'proof' was easily produced. A singer who had been entertaining them was not so lucky. She was taken away to another police station where she was found guilty of being improperly dressed – wearing tight trousers – and given forty lashes.

Encountering such a wide spectrum of behaviour, belief and standard of living among just three families, living within a radius of 100 metres from me, was intriguing. Getting to know the converts was even more so.

4 ISLAM IN SUDAN

Talking with the converts stimulated in me a renewed interest in the country I had been living in for four years. I began to realise that I had only a superficial knowledge of what I was fast discovering was a complex and fascinating culture. Nor did I really know all that much about Islam, despite having previously worked in Muslim environments in Iraq, Zanzibar and Malaysia.

In Malaysia, out of interest, I attended a course in Islam designed for people who were converting. Basically this meant non–Muslims, mainly Koreans, who were marrying Muslim Malays and had to convert before being allowed to do so.

With Haji Amza, a former army man who now had some kind of religious job, we went through the five pillars, the ten angels and the twenty–five Prophets. Then somebody else joined the class and we had to go back to the beginning again. When another new person came after we'd been over the five pillars and the ten angels for the second time, we again returned to square one. We never did get very far.

To make matters worse Haji Amza's English wasn't very good and he often had difficulty in explaining things. When questioned further he would refer people to me. "Ask Mister Hilda. She have a very good knowledge of the Koran." This can only have been because my English was up to the task because I certainly didn't know much about the Koran. Like many non–Arabic–speaking non–Muslims I found it difficult to engage with it.

In addition to being familiar with the five pillars, the angels, the Prophets and the life of Mohammed, I knew how Muslims were supposed to behave, that they were divided into two main branches – Sunni and Shia – that the fundamentalists of Saudi Arabia were Wahhabis, and that some Muslims were Sufis. That was about it.

I now started on a steep learning curve.

Nowadays, Sudanese Muslims cover the full range of Islamic belief, from extremist Wahhabi–type groups to moderate and tolerant individuals who subscribe to no particular agenda. The majority of Northern Sudanese belong to the latter category, with many of them being members of the various Sufi sects (*tariqas*).

Like most foreigner visitors to Khartoum I had gone to see the whirling dervishes at Hamed al Niel mosque in Omdurman, one of Sudan's best–known tourist attractions. Every Friday afternoon a great crowd gathers to watch as followers of Sheikh Hamdu Niil appear in the distance, dressed in garish green and red gowns, and slowly approach the mosque *en masse*, chanting, swaying and spinning in an elaborate Sufi ritual. This so–called dervish dancing is really a form of Sufi worship, a means of generating a state of religious ecstasy and bringing about a closer union with God. The Hamed Al Niel *zikr* is one of the more spectacular examples of a form of worship which is carried out, usually in a more sober fashion, by hundreds of thousands of Muslims throughout Sudan, and by Sufis throughout the world.

Although a near neighbour of Saudi Arabia – the cradle of Islam – which lies just at the other side of the Red Sea, Northern Sudan did not become predominantly Muslim until the forteenth and fifteenth centuries. The orthodox Sunni missionaries who came first were followed by a number of Sufi holy men – *faki* – who taught that the way to spiritual fulfilment is through mystical experience and it is this brand of Islam that is most widely followed in Sudan today. The word *sufi* comes from the Arabic word *suf* – wool – referring to the simple woollen garment worn by early Islamic ascetics.

Sufism developed early on in the history of Islam as a

reaction against the increasing formalism of orthodox Islam and its obsession with laws and procedural matters. It emphasises the inner dimension of religion, the relationship between the individual and God. Sufis seek direct personal experience of God through special spiritual practices. These exercises (*zikr*) involve the prolonged recital of prayers, passages from the Koran, and the names and attributes of God. At the same time the devotee carries out a prescribed series of physical movements, the aim being to induce a transcendental state which will take him into the presence of God and allow him to feel his love.

Although many orthodox Muslims disapprove of Sufi practices, Sufism is not a separate branch of Islam in the way that the Shia tradition is different from the Sunni. Sudanese Sufis, like other Sudanese Muslims and the great majority of Muslims worldwide, follow the Sunni tradition. The *tariqas* are comparable rather to the various Catholic guilds or lay brotherhoods; it is a discipline or lifestyle adopted in addition to one's basic religious beliefs.

A Sufi *tariqa* binds together groups of people who follow a spiritual path under the guidance of a master, or sheikh. Historically, these sheikhs have always played a leading role as spiritual leaders in community life in Sudan, particularly in the countryside. They are also believed to possess special powers – *baraka* – enabling them to cure diseases and perform miracles.

"Almost every locality had a sheikh who gained fame, usually by his knowledge, by his piety, by his ability to settle quarrels between couples, quarrels between families or quarrels between tribes," says Griselda. "This was the role of the local *faki*, that he was above all worldly politics and worldly gain and he was knowledgeable about the Koran and he could play the role of the mediator, of the spiritual leader, of the person that everybody trusted. Worldly politics would come and go, the khedival armies would come and go, but the local sheikhs were the focus of what people felt they could relate to."

The various fundamentalist groups which have appeared more recently are, she believes, a foreign import.

"The *Ansar al Sunna* have been influenced by the Wahhabis of Saudi Arabia but they are, as it were, foreign. They've come from the outside and they're kind of grafted on to the body politic of this country, but the cult of the local sheikh, several governments have tried to defeat it and they haven't been able to. The NIF is all–powerful in government now but in the villages and in the rural areas the local sheikhs have still managed to get local support and local following."

Griselda contrasts the position of the Sudanese sheikhs with the mullahs in Iran. "There is a big difference between them and the mullahs, who have tremendous power. In a way the whole history of Sudan goes against these sheikhs having too much political power. They have spiritual power."

Belief in this power has led to the cult of the saint developing among the religious brotherhoods in Sudan, as elsewhere in African Islam. Evidence of this can be seen in the form of the many saints' tombs – squat square buildings topped with beehive–shaped domes – which dot the countryside. Although orthodox Islam frowns on this kind of thing, the tombs become the focus of pilgrimage and prayer. Followers believe that the *baraka* a sheikh possesses in life increases after death, putting him in an even stronger position to intercede for them with God.

At a more practical level the *tariqas* provide yet more cohesive glue in a society which already has strong relationship networks in the form of family and tribal commitment.

"In Sudan *tariqa*s cut across tribal structure and family and clans," says Griselda. "A person belongs first to the family, then the clan, then the tribe. Belonging to a sect enables you to relate to people who do not belong to the same family or tribe. Family comes first for questions of marriage but the *tariqa*'s more important for jobs. *Tariqas* are a bit like houses in public schools. They have ranks, like captains and majors, a bit like the Freemasons."

There are no doctrinal differences between the Sufi sects. Membership of one *tariqa* rather than other is a matter of personal preference for the type of spiritual practice adopted or for the way in which the *tariqa* is organised.

Jane Anne's husband, Yazin, is a *Sammaniya*, while his mother is a *Khatimiya* and his father a member of the more extreme Ansari sect.

"I chose it myself because of the ways of practising," says Yazin. "This is a group of people I like and this is a group of people I would feel good being among. It doesn't matter what social class you are, when you're together you're like one family.".

"You can't find a single house in Sudan without a member connected with the *tasawwuf*," Sheikh Hassan Qaribullah said to me.

Sheikh Qaribullah was dressed in a full–length moss–coloured cloak with a beige embroidered shawl round his shoulders. He had eyes which seemed to both glow and twinkle at the same time. A little crescent of short white hairs garnished his chin.

We moved on to theological matters. As we discussed his arguments against Jesus being divine, a tray of refreshments – a jug of *abreh* and a glass of mint tea – was set out on a little table beside me, served with the deftness and exquisite courtesy you might expect in a Michelin five star. The Sheikh himself took nothing as he was fasting, a regular discipline he imposes on himself in addition to the normal Ramadan fast.

The Sheikh is a leader of the *Sammaniya* sect, the largest Sufi *tariqa* in Sudan. He is descended from the sheikh who introduced the sect from Saudi Arabia where it was founded in the 18th century by Samman, a Muslim mystic in Medina.

Sheikh Qaribulla has a number of Western followers, particularly British. Every year many of them come to Sudan to celebrate *Laylat el Gadar*, the last ten days of Ramadan. Many Muslims believe that whatever wish you ask God for will be granted on one of these days. At Sheikh Qaribulla's mosque *Laylat el Gadar* starts with a night of exuberant *zikr* with groups from different *tariqas*, each performing its own worship ritual. Crowds of people attend, either as spectators or dancing and chanting and drumming all night long. There is a fairground atmosphere, with food stalls, vendors of religious paraphernalia and a big tent crammed with pictures, books and other items related to the sect and its sheikhs.

I had hoped that Sheikh Qaribulla might be able to tell me something about his foreign followers but he was strangely uninformed about them. Although the people who come for the *Laylat el Gadar* are accommodated in the guest house attached to the mosque no one asks them for any personal details, not even their names or their country of origin. "All are welcome," said the Sheikh. "No questions are asked." It seemed an unusually *laissez–faire* attitude in a country where you could not set foot outside the capital without a travel permit or spend a night anywhere without registering with the police.

I asked Sheikh Qaribulla why so many Western converts came to Sudan.

"The tolerance of the Sudanese could explain this," he replied. "The Sudanese respect foreigners, more than people in other countries. And the Sudanese are so honest."

I later attended a *zikr* in the Sheikh Qaribulla mosque. The ceremony, which lasts for about five or six hours, looked like a blend of aerobics and bioenergetics. Several hundred men, all wearing white *jellabiya*s and the distinctive wide brown leather belt of the Sammaniya with a bandolier across the right shoulder, were lined up on both sides of the street in front of the mosque. Sheikh Qaribullah stood in the centre, orchestrating the procedure like a circus ring–master. The men swayed repeatedly from left to right, breathing hard. After a while they started to jump up and down. Then they switched to a bending movement, swooping low from the waist. They followed this with a turning back motion, throwing the arm over as if picking something up from behind. The pattern of movements was accompanied by a variety of sounds: a mournful singing, a series of escalating grunts, a breathing of words which could barely be heard. "La illaha illa allah." There is no god but God.

After watching the men – from a distance, as they don't really like women to be present at all – I went inside the mosque where the women were participating from behind the external wall. The atmosphere here was different, more informal and relaxed. Of the sixty or so women present, about half were lined up performing the same ritual as the men. The other half wandered around or sat about chatting. Seeing me sitting behind them, several of those taking part indicated that I should join in. Propelled by a lot of good–natured shoving by both participants and spectators I gave it a go. I lasted about ten minutes before becoming disoriented and dizzy. From the other side of the wall the pace of the chanting was accelerating and the volume of sound was rising. The *zikr* was approaching its climax.

Michael Metcalfe, a British convert living in Sudan, describes the experience as inducing a sense of unity with Allah. "I have personal contact with Allah all the time. I see Allah as being transcendant *and* immanent. That's what I perceive the whole Sufi thing as being about. I've never seen God as this William Blake thing."

Although he enjoys taking part in the *zikr* and has great praise for Sheikh Qaribulla, Michael is not a member of the *tariqa*. "I try to stop myself from becoming 'insectified'," he says with a laugh.

Sheikh Qaribullah is only one of several high profile Sudanese sheikhs who attract a foreign following. Another is Sheikh Ibrahim Muhammad Uthman, a leader of the Burhaniya *tariqa* which has followers throughout Europe and other parts of the world, but particularly in Germany where they have a thriving centre.

I visited Sheikh Ibrahim in his villa in Riyadh, an upmarket suburb of Khartoum, with a Sudanese friend, Maha. We had gone looking for him at his mosque near Khartoum Race Course and had been told that we should just go and drop in on him at his house.

It was just about time for a *majlis*, a kind of come–one–come–all group reception. We waited outside in the garden with other visitors, mainly women, most of whom were praying fervently, passing the beads of an Islamic 'rosary' through their fingers as they recited the ninety–nine names of Allah.

We were all taken upstairs and then up into a slightly raised mezzanine area where Sheikh Ibrahim sat on a plush sheepskin–covered armchair. His feet rested on a low stool. A *huwar* massaged them throughout the time we were there.

As a foreigner I was treated as a guest of honour – the focus of the conversation and the first to be served with tea. For the benefit of the others present we spoke in Arabic, with Maha translating.

Sheikh Ibrahim seemed to be something of a globe–trotting showman. He spoke in an oratorical way as if addressing a much larger audience, describing the success of the Burhaniya *tariqa* worldwide and his own part in it. His replies to my questions seemed to lack spontaneity, as if he had searched through a range of pre–prepared answers to find the nearest thing relating to what I wanted to know, producing something that was always a bit off–topic.

I had heard that he was a specialist in conversion and his stories seemed to bear this out, though I could not understand what it was about him or his ideas that would seduce non–believers. He talked of an overnight boat trip from England to Sweden during which he had converted three Swedes. "By the time we reached Gothenburg in the morning they had all recited the *shahada*," he claimed. It all seemed a bit too glib. "Tell her I'll convert her now," he said to Maha, although I had given no indication of being in the least interested in becoming a Muslim.

I later spoke with Safwat Singer, the *tariqa*'s public relations officer. We met in his office, a smart building opposite the mosque, well fitted out with the latest in computer equipment.

Safwat was a small, rotund Egyptian. He was wearing an

orange skull cap instead of the usual white. He was warm and voluble, eager to promote Sufism as being the real Islam, which he believes corresponds to what it was in the time of the Prophet. He claims that until the introduction of Wahhabism by Nimeiri in the 1980s about 90 per cent of Sudanese Muslims were Sufi.

"The ideas of countries like Saudi Arabia are not the real meaning of Islam. For people like that it is just based on beard for man and *emma* and short *jellibiya*," he said, referring to the practice of the more extreme male Muslims of imitating the Prophet by wearing a beard and dressing in the same way as he did. "And for women like this." He made a miming gesture to indicate being clothed from head to toe. "Islam is not like this."

The Sufi brand of Islam is, he believes, much more attractive to Westerners and potential converts. "In Germany we have a small *zawiya*. Lots of Germans joined us in the first six months. The Saudis have a big mosque nearby. They've been there for ten years but they have no Germans."

Every year the Burhaniya mosque in Khartoum holds a celebration, a *houliya*, attended by believers from all over the world, including large numbers from Germany and Scandinavain countries. Guests are accommodated in a school nearby and in the houses of local Burhaniyas, and follow a programme of religious, social and tourist activities.

"It is no problem for us, we have been doing this *houliya* for twenty years," Safwat told me. "We have buses for them to come here and to return to their houses. And for the food, for everything we arrange, it is no problem. They stay between seven days and fifteen days. They have their daily programme. They do *salat* in the mosque, they visit the *Maulana*. If there is somebody wants to go shopping, somebody goes with him for the shopping. There are trips for them on the Nile river. And after they return between *salat al maghrib* and *salat al isha*, always there is a lecture for them. After the *salat al isha* there is the *zikr*, generally until midnight, and they return to their homes."

While we were talking a tall black American of wraith–like

33

thinness flitted into the room. He wore a ragged *jellabiya* over frayed trousers and had an Andy Capp style of cloth cap on top of his white skull cap. He flopped on to a chair, fingering his prayer beads, and started talking about his passport.

Safwat introduced us. "This is Rashad, from America. He's been staying with us for a few weeks."

We spoke briefly about his visit to Sudan. Rashad's face wore an unchanging beatific smile. His tone of voice alternated between challenging and weary. Just as suddenly as he had come in, he stood up and drifted out again.

"He is psychologically ill," Safwat explained. "We are looking after him."

The prevalence of Sufi values in Sudan, and the moderate and tolerant character of the Sudanese people do not seem to accord with the hardline stance of the government and the growth of extremist groups such as the Muslim Brotherhood and the *Ansar al Sunna*. How can the two sides co–exist?

Griselda points out that the Sudanese always manage to find ways round the excessive Islam imposed on them by the government. "When the police clamped down on discos in clubs, they were simply moved to private houses," she says. "The Sudanese are very pious when it comes to praying and fasting but a lot of drinking goes on and it always has. There's probably a Muslim school of thought which thinks it's OK to drink but not to get drunk. And working within the rules of the dress code, women can still make themselves look attractive. You just have to look at all these carefully matched colour combinations, for example, the kind of thing the girls are all wearing now – the smart skirt and the toning blouse and *tarha*."

This was true. The dress code of clothes down to the ankles and wrists and head covered, when translated into pencil skirt, waist–clinching shirt and light scarf over the head with half the hair showing, could be far more seductive than sleeveless tee shirts and mini–skirts or frayed jeans.

Griselda believes that social and moral attitudes change in a cyclical way. "People get decadent and they indulge in gambling and drinking and this, that and the other and then there comes a reformist, and then there's a puritanic revolution. It's like Britain with Oliver Cromwell and then the Victorians and then the Methodists. We seem to have these cycles of decadence and permissive society and then a reform, then people get fed up. Can't you see it building up now that people are thinking that drinks are going to come back to Khartoum?"

Griselda was referring to the unofficial relaxation of rules that had come about as the peace talks advanced, the feeling that there was a bit more give on the part of the authorities and that more was to come.

"Can't you feel it in the air? The girls are wearing much more daring clothes than they were a year or two ago, their skirts so tight–fitting and so on."

Generally the Sudanese have no inhibitions about expressing their opinions privately. There isn't the feeling that they're looking over their shoulders all the time that you might find in some countries.

Omar, a Sudanese translator in his 50s, sees the government's move towards a harsher application of Islamic rules in the past twenty years as being motivated by political expediency, a sop to the more fundamentalist groups to win their loyalty.

"It was a strategy. You play the game their way – the people of the fringe, the extremists, the ultra–fundamentalists, the *Takfiri*, the *Tablighi*, the *Ansar al Sunna*, whatever that's within the orthodox Muslim school of thought – if you hang up their slogans, if you put whatever they're preaching into practice in acts and legislation, I think you're telling them, look, I am enacting what you're preaching."

There was no risk of this backfiring with the moderates, he believes. By their very nature they are not going to rise in revolt, whereas the extremists, if not placated, could be a threat.

"The Sufis won't politically go against something like a dress code, however outrageous it might be. You're a Sufi, yes, of course you shake hands with women, of course you don't care about how your own daughters are dressed, but you can't go publicly and say no, what you're doing in terms of dress code and banning music is against what I believe in. You have to shut up and do your things your way. You use the music in your *zikr*, the government will turn a blind eye to that and in exchange you have to shut up. You can't go on television and say this is against Islam as I see it. You can't say, I'm a Sufi and I don't think the government has any business determining to people what they should or shouldn't wear."

Professor Tigani Hassan, Director of the Faith Research Centre in Khartoum, sees this same divide between the government and the governed. "You will notice that in Sudan the people don't bend their heads to any ruler. He may have his own drum and beat it and dance to it but the people do what they are convinced to do. The net result right now is that there is a disparity between what is said and what is practised."

This was a point I found being made time and again: the difference between what the government say, want and profess to believe, and what the people say, want and believe.

"We no longer believe that they can be our custodians to talk about Islam," Professor Tigani went on, "because the true Islam, the Sufi Islam, is not the Islam that is practised at government level. The government is trying its best now to make good relations with the Sufis because of course, after all, the majority of the people are there."

5 RELIGIOUS BELIEFS AND PRACTICES

For non–Muslims the ideas that most commonly spring to mind when Islam is mentioned are the sensational ones: polygamy, judicial amputations, the stoning of adulterers, veiled women. On the whole, these are not big issues in Sudan.

Despite the fundamentalism of the government, the outward face of Sudan is very different from that of, say, Saudi Arabia. There is no Chop Square as there is in Riyadh and fully veiled women are relatively rare. Even when *sharia* law was being most severely imposed, its application incorporated a modicum of mercy; amputation was generally the sentence of last resort, in cases where there were no extenuating circumstances or legal loopholes to allow a lesser punishment. As a signatory to several international conventions which implicitly outlaw these punishments, Sudan has agreed to abolish them although there has been evidence in recent years that courts in some parts of the country have been breaching this undertaking.

Polygamy

Westerners are generally horrified at the idea of a man having more than one wife, believing that it victimises the women concerned. It's often used as the basis for a jibe at men converting to Islam – *Oh, he just wants to have several wives* – ignoring the fact that if he remained a non–Muslim he could still have one wife and several mistresses which would probably be a lot cheaper. Or ridicule is poured on the idea that anyone could actually fulfil the requirement that must be met: that all wives must be treated equally. This seems as impossible as Portia's stipulation that Shylock should take no more and no less than one pound of flesh.

Abdel Karim has the full conjugal allowance. I met two of his wives when I attended a *yom as samaya* celebration for the new–born daughter of Abu Bakr, a Nigerian friend.

When I arrived at Abu's house he took me straight through the sitting room where the men were and directed me into a curtained off section at the end. Abu's wife and a few other women were there, lounging on *angaraibs*, all of them dressed in ample full–length dresses and veils. Their *niqabs* were tossed back over their heads, ready to be brought down again as soon as they found themselves in the presence of a man.

We stayed there while the men went outside for the naming ceremony. While the men named the baby and passed her round from one to the other praying over her, inside we got round to talking about being a co–wife.

Ishraga, a tall, graceful and very beautiful woman, was Abdel Karim's second wife. They had met while he was teaching in a language school, she told me. She was one of his pupils. When he proposed to her she had accepted willingly. The fact that he already had a wife presented no problem for her. Her family were less happy about the idea of her becoming a co–wife but she persuaded them to agree to it. Ishraga lived with Abdel Karim and his first wife, who wasn't there. She had stayed at home with her baby. The third wife, Miriam, a rather plain woman with bad skin, was exceptionally devout. Her relationship with Abdel Karim had developed because of their common interest in discussing religious matters, she explained. Miriam had not been keen when Abdel Karim first suggested marriage to her but she had allowed herself to be persuaded when he told her he was motivated by the feeling that he could learn a lot from her about Islam. Since their marriage she had continued to live at home with her mother and sister.

At midday all the women laid out mats and prayed. After going through the set procedures the other women rolled up their mats, settled back on the beds and resumed their conversations. Miriam carried on praying. She knelt on the floor, sitting back on her heels, praying out loud and gazing upwards as if seeing a vision. Later she perched on the edge of a bed, alternately reading from the Koran and talking to Allah as if in a trance. When we left in the evening I walked to the bus with Kahlil and his two wives. Ishraga, Abdel Karim and I talked but Miriam read from the Koran as she walked along.

Abdel Karim is a staunch defender of polygamy (or polygyny, to give it the more accurate name which he prefers, as Islam allows men to have more than one spouse but not women). He believes it should be encouraged not only for Muslims but for non–Muslims too.

"Many social problems stem from one–parent families," he says. "Marriage to more than one woman should be legal so that these children can have two parents. Legal changes have been made to accommodate shifts in attitude to other issues – for example the decriminalisation of homosexuality, the legalisation of gay marriage in some countries, the movement to decriminalise the use of soft drugs – so why not similar action to legalise polygamy for those who want it?

"What I'm advocating is that men who choose to have relationships should be responsible for those relationships. The law in Britain chooses to have child support care whether the man is married or not. What they want is money. It's hypocrisy. You can't on the one hand say if you choose to take another wife and live with her we're going to put you in jail but any offspring that comes from this woman we expect you to pay for it. It's incredibly unreasonable. My advocacy of this issue is quite clear, that the question of polygyny should be made available to solve social ills, throughout the Western hemisphere as well as in Muslim countries," he says.

The two wives I had been speaking to seemed happy with

the arrangement. Abdel Karim saw no reason why other women should not be equally agreeable to it, though the arguments he gives may not hold as much water in societies where labour–saving devices and the sharing of household tasks between man and wife are more common than in Sudan.

"The benefits for the women are immense. We live in a society today where, especially in Muslim societies, women are very pressed to undertake the services for their husbands. Every day they should be cooking and cleaning and washing. This also in some cases obviates the ability for a woman to educate herself, a situation where women are not able to educate themselves because they're getting married very early, straight away being thrown into having children and having to cater for a husband. In the question of polygyny where a woman shares the responsibilities for her husband it leaves her opportunities far more open".

There still remains the question of how one man is to support four wives.

"It is incumbent upon a man to provide for his wife from the staple diet of the country. So therefore if he is rich he's required to provide two handfuls – in Sudan one can say of *ful*, which is broad beans. One might find this extraordinary that that's all he's obliged to provide but that's in fact all. Two handfuls of *ful* a day with something to cook it. If you look at the schools of Islam you find in Shafi it quite clearly states this, in Maliki also."

Abdel Karim was referring to the four major schools of thought relating to Islamic jurisprudence founded by *imam*s ibn Hanbal, abu Hanifa, Malek, and el Shafei during the 9th to 11th centuries. They are known as the Hanbali, Hanafi, Maliki and Shafei schools. The schools differ in their interpretation of the *sharia* but all are recognised as valid. Muslims refer to them for guidance on how to behave. The Maliki is the one generally followed in Sudan.

Abdel Karim went on to say that for a poor man the minimum obligation is to provide only one handful of *ful* a day.

"Under most circumstances one is able to provide much more than that. We've got to a situation where people understand that provision entails extravagance but Islam goes back to the essentials and essentially people can live if they're forced to on this amount of food per day. I'm sure this sounds extraordinary. It will sound unfair. It will sound amazing but when one has a responsibility for four wives, OK, then four handfuls is actually not very much."

With regard to the requirement that the husband should treat all his wives equally Abdel Karim doesn't see this as a problem because he believes that the question of fairness only comes into play in the amount of time a man spends with his wives. It doesn't mean that he has to love them equally.

"The amount of time that you spend with your wives has to be rigorously fair. This is what is meant by the item in the Koran about fairness and justice. But logically if one wife is pleasant, she deals with you in a very nice way, she makes sure that you are happy and you make sure that she's happy. There's a cooperation between you. And quite naturally one's heart would be far more open to a person whose heart is open to you.

"The quality of the time of course is something that depends on her and you. The question of fairness does not enter into the quality. Some wives, you sit there and try to make conversation with them and they don't. Others will find that they only need you when they want you to provide something for the children. Others will want to have intellectual conversations about situations and politics etc. So the quality of the time depends solely on the relationship between your wife and you. The question about how you feel, if you love one wife more than another, again this doesn't enter the question of fairness.... The requirement in Islam is that in no way should any feeling of rancour that you might have about your wife at one point or another mean that you should deprive her of the time that is rightly hers."

Mohammed Abdul Qaadir married his first wife recently and hopes to have at least one more.

"I don't know how many, whatever Allah blesses me to do. It is the *sunna* of Prophet Mohammed to marry four but if he blesses me to take two, then I'll take two. This is an example of how in a society when you have more women than men, and you have this trend of many women being educated but not being married, a man marrying more than one wife can help society. There will be all of those women who are unmarried because they've spent most of their time seeking education and now they're 30 years old and no longer desirable by a man any more. In Sudan, you know, once a woman reaches say 22, 24 she's not the most desirable. They tend to marry younger women. Sudanese like to flirt with the girls in the university but when it comes down to getting married they go back to their village or they will marry someone from their home."

"I'm now gearing towards the woman who is educated in order to have someone to help me to educate my children. I don't want to send them to the Sudanese government schools so my dilemma is – how do I educate my children?"

"My present wife will help me but it will be more in terms of character, not academically. I mean, she would not be able to help my children in Arabic language or geography or mathematics. I would be interested in marrying a woman who has studied at Omdurman University, either in the Islamic sciences or the Arabic language. Omdurman University traditionally has been educating women and men according to Islamic principles and it is not gender integrated."

Su'ad, a woman who works on Jane Anne's farm, is a co–wife.

"A lot of them have two or three wives," Jane Anne says. "What happened with Su'ad was El Hady's other wife wasn't respecting him, so he married Su'ad. At a certain stage in a marriage your children become more important than your husband. Your children are part of you, you've given birth to them and you spend more of your time with them, and of course you love them more because they've come from you; you've only *married* your husband. So there comes a time in the marriage when the husband feels very left out and the woman's tired all the time and he can't have what he wants every night and things like that. So an easy way out for the Sudanese is they marry another wife. They get a new bride; they're getting their hanky–panky every night, she's not tired because she hasn't got any kids. What happens is he spends a lot of attention on her so the other wife gets jealous and then when they go to the other wife they have good things with the other wife as well so they have good things on both sides. It all boils down to S–E–X. That's what it all boils down to. El Hady's living at the farm with Su'ad. He only goes to the first wife three nights, that's nights from eight o'clock at night to four o'clock in the morning so she doesn't have to put up with him all day. She also had two children after he married Su'ad so you're not telling me they're not enjoying themselves. But when he goes to her she's not tired because she hasn't had him all day, she doesn't have to cook for him, she doesn't have to wash and iron his clothes for him. She's pleased to see him, she wants to show she's pleased to see him because he spends all his time with Su'ad, so he enjoys himself with her. And then he comes back to Su'ad. She's jealous because he's been there so she looks after him. It's a way of the men getting themselves looked after. It's always after a certain amount of years' marriage that they marry another one."

Of all the Sudanese men I knew there was only one, as far as I was aware, who had more than one wife. He was a man in his 50s, well off, with a large house divided into two flats, one for each of the wives. They didn't like the arrangement, he told me, but put up with each other. I started to ask around to find out how common polygyny was.

"It used to be common, among older people," said Omar. "In the olden days it wouldn't cost much to have a couple of kids with a wife in Shendi and another wife in Khartoum with four or five, but I don't see that this is quite possible for the vast number of men under 40 who have never yet got married."

I asked him what Sudanese people would think about Abdel Karim and Khalid.

"The older ones like myself would simply say, well, lucky them. I mean, I have no idea of getting married again, of having a second wife, but if the wives are satisfied and happy, why not? The younger people, I think, would look at it in a different way. They definitely wouldn't be of the same view as our generation. In our upbringing if a man had one wife his colleagues and his peers used to tease him. It was common that they tease people like, oh, you're a single wife type. It was like a laughing stock, something for teasing. You're not remarrying because you're not man enough or whatever."

Kamal, who is about twenty years younger, disagreed with the view that polygamy is dying out.

"Polygamy has been in Sudan since ages but now it's gaining ground more, not among all people, but the rich and specially the *nouveau riche*. It's like a sort of entertainment. I've got the money, why not have another wife? But it's not common in the sense... for example, among my friends, I hardly have two or three, out of say fifty, who have more than one wife. In fact, there is another problem, people in their 30s not getting married at all. It's more common to find someone who hasn't married and who is 40. And there are many women who are ready to marry even, as we call it, a second–hand husband, as a co–wife. Most of the songs, you know these girls' songs, they mention it. Like, I'm looking for a way to get rid of my present situation of celibacy and I'm even ready to marry a man who's got another wife."

Deirdre, a British woman married to a Sudanese, recalled discussing the subject with a group of female students and finding that opinions were divided. "A number said they wanted to be married to men who were married, or had been married before. They said such men made better husbands as they knew how to deal with women. The majority though were against it."

Hudud punishments

The harsh applications of *sharia* law shock non–Muslims. Although the more severe *hudud* punishments have supposedly been suspended in Sudan, amputation sentences were still being handed out at the time of writing.

Human Rights Watch and Sudan Victims of Torture Group reported numerous cases of amputation and cross–amputation (right hand and left leg) in 2002. In that year also fourteen women in the west of Sudan were sentenced to 100 lashes for adultery. An 18–year–old non–Muslim Dinka woman was sentenced to death by stoning for the same crime, but had the sentence reduced on appeal to seventy–five lashes. Of eighty–eight people sentenced to death in Darfur in July of that year, two were 14–year–old boys.

Deirdre had her car stolen shortly after *sharia* law was introduced. The thief was caught and Deirdre had to attend the trial. To her relief the judge was able to impose a lesser punishment as Deirdre had facilitated the theft by her carelessness. "I was glad the judge gave the thief every chance to say I'd made it easy for him to steal it by leaving half an inch of window open. Otherwise he would have been eligible for amputation and I would have had to attend. I'd left the little gap so the car wouldn't explode with the heat."

In mid–2003 the case of a Muslim woman, Safiyatu Huseini Tugur–Tudu was receiving international media attention. A divorcee, she had been condemned to death by stoning in Nigeria for having sexual relations with a man who was not her husband. The sentence had been postponed until she weaned the child which had resulted from the union. This time was now near and final appeals were being heard in the court.

I asked Mohammed Abdul Qaadir if he felt uncomfortable with the idea of stoning a woman to death.

"Not at all. This is Islam. I believe Islam to be the perfect religion in that the Koran is the word of God and I believe the

45

Koran to be the perfect book and it is the word of God and the word of God could not be imperfect."

The Islamic *sharia* is based on what is written in the Koran and on the words and actions of Prophet Mohammed. Mohammed quoted the case of a woman who had transgressed in a similar way at the time of the Prophet.

"It was clear that she had committed fornication with a man. This woman was pregnant. She came to the Prophet in repentance of her action, because she wanted to be punished, because she realised that it was better to be punished in this life rather than in the next life. Because the punishment in this life of being killed would be very little, would be minute, insignificant compared with the punishment after death, she realised it would simply be better to accept her punishment in this life. However she was pregnant so the Prophet said no, go and give birth to your child and then come back. From what I understand, they would not necessarily have sought her out if she hadn't come back. But she did come back and she was then told to breastfeed her child to the point where he no longer needed the mother's services. She came back after having done so and she was executed.

"It's not explicit what Muslims should do necessarily but there are those scholars of Islam who understand the Koranic judgement, the sayings and acts of Prophet Mohammed, and they are able to delineate what should be done in these cases."

Hijab

Although it probably has less impact on the lives of the women concerned than polygamy or *hudud* punishment, the *hijab* must be one of the Islamic issues most talked about by non–Muslims. Unlike polygamy, which is illegal in most non–Muslim countries, and *hudud* punishments which are even more restricted, the *hijab* question arises in some way or other wherever Muslim women are to be found.

It was receiving particular attention in Europe towards the end of 2003 as France prepared to pass legislation to ban the wearing of the *hijab* in state schools. Around the same time a French bank came in for criticism when a guard refused access to a woman wearing a *hijab* as he considered it a security risk. The bank defended itself by saying that all customers were required to take off head coverings as a measure against robbers trying to disguise themselves.

The French move was intended to promote secularisation by banning religious symbols, and included also Jewish skullcaps, Sikh turbans and Christian crosses. But for those Muslims who believe it is ordained in the Koran, the *hijab* is not a symbol, it is an obligation. Going without it is, to them, indecent. Being told to take it off would be comparable to another woman being told to take off her skirt.

Commentators in the British media criticised France for its rigid stance and praised Britain as a more open society where people of other faiths had freedom to practise their religions. But around the same time a girl in Luton was taking her school to court for refusing to allow her to wear the *jilbab* (long Muslim cloak) and a teacher in Peterborough was cleared of religiously aggravated assault for pulling the *hijab* off the head of a pupil.

Lena Winfrey, who used to wear mini–skirts and black nail polish and have her hair dyed pink, tells of her mother's reaction when she converted to Islam and started wearing the *hijab*.

"I didn't cover in the first part of being a Muslim. I just dressed modestly, long skirts, no make–up, and then I had to tell my parents because I was writing an article in the local newspaper about Ramadan and my father would read it and I didn't want it to be such a shock for him to read that I was a Muslim without me telling him. So I told my mother by telephone and she was crying and couldn't understand why and where she went wrong and I told her 'no, you went right'. Then after that I wanted to wear the Islamic dress which was about three weeks after I told them I was a Muslim and then I told my mother by telephone that I had put on the *hijab* and she hung up on me. I called back and then she said it was bad enough that you took that religion but why did you have to put that towel on your head? And she said, what will the neighbours think? I told her, I don't care what the neighbours think. So she was more concerned about what the neighbours were thinking, not that I'd changed my religion. So after that I came to visit them and my father was laughing at me because of my dress and he wanted to take a picture."

Outside the family it marked her out for discrimination and insults.

"When I put on the *hijab* in America it was as if I was putting on another skin colour. I really have an understanding of what the black people went through in America and how people were racist against them. From the beginning when I started wearing my *hijab* I would go places and people would laugh at me. They would just burst out laughing, and staring. Sometimes they would snicker and make a comment, like: Are you cold? And they would whistle, you know, like trying to pick you up, they would beep–beep from the car."

This is one of the reasons Lena feels much more at ease in Sudan.

"Here what I do like is that the government is leading them towards Islam. Here I'm free to practise my Islam and if I want to be religious or I want to wear *hijab* it's encouraged, it's very normal."

Michael Metcalfe has no doubts about the desirability of women keeping their heads covered.

At the time we spoke Michael shared a house with two young British women who taught in the same school as he did. The women had integrated well into Sudanese life with the exception that their dress code was at total variance with that in force among Sudanese women. Sleeveless tops, short skirts slit above the knee, and the stretch of bare midriff that was in fashion at the time. On one occasion as I sat with him one of the women came out of the shower and walked past us wearing nothing but a towel which covered her from mid–thigh to armpits.

But Michael says: "I agree with *hijab*. I agree totally with it. I've got no qualms about it. If I ever marry again my wife would have to wear *hijab*. Without it, that's bad, it's not nice. I'm not what you'd call strict but I know in my mind what's right."

Niqab

The *hijab* refers only to the head veil. Some women go further and cover their faces with the *niqab*. Mohammed Abdul Qaadir would like his wife to wear this although she herself is not willing.

"Originally when we got married I wanted her to wear the *niqab*. She did at first. She found it difficult of course, people in Sudan don't like it generally, but there are many people that do. Then her mother said it would be OK for her to take it off. Although it was important to me I didn't push the issue just to avoid problems. But now I will ask her again to wear it. She doesn't want to necessarily, it won't be her desire, but she will wear it. I have no intention of forcing her, it's just that it's my preference due to the times that we live in where the religiousness of the people has gone, where you find men who are very rude in their looking at women and very disrespectful. I'm pretty confident that she will not fuss about it. My wife is, *alhamdullila*, very obedient."

6 TRADITIONAL BELIEFS AND PRACTICES

"Culture and tradition override Islam here. They pervade it. Last night I said: 'I don't want to shake hands with women' and they laughed at me."

Michael Metcalfe, who has a degree in Arabic language and political Islam, was complaining about the extent to which Islam in Sudan is polluted by elements from traditional behaviours and beliefs.

"I lived in Yemen for two years so that shapes my thought. Particularly the stance with women. In Yemen the segregation is absolute. Here it's African Islam. I'm coming to this from a very different angle. I'm an Arabist, with preconceived Arab norms."

Mohammed Abdul Qaadir has similar reservations. "Being that the Sudanese are so friendly, the most religious men and the most religious women still observe the Sudanese traditions, for example, shaking hands, which is clearly forbidden in Islam. But it's a big tradition for the Sudanese and they are unwilling to leave it."

For people with such views there are bound to be difficulties about life in Sudan, both at the social level and in the way people express their spiritual beliefs. It was for this kind of reason that the two American women at BEI went back home after just a few months.

The Sudanese are traditionally friendly and tolerant. Most see nothing wrong in men shaking hands with women. Although there is a certain amount of polarisation of the two sexes, they generally mix quite readily. And, were the *hijab* not imposed by the government, many women would go about with their heads uncovered.

Weddings

The ways in which the Sudanese conduct the rituals associated with major life events can also attract criticism from purists. Sudanese weddings, for example, last several days and include different ceremonies, some of which seem to flout rules of orthodox Islamic behaviour. In one of them, the bride dances for a female audience, usually wearing very revealing clothes. Originally the bride would have been naked for this, except for a leather fringed skirt, to allow her in–laws to check that she had no deformities. The dancing itself is sexually suggestive and is made more so by the words of the accompanying songs. The husband watches, brandishing a sword. At a certain point he must try to stop her falling to the ground. If he fails, she is said to have scored a goal which means that she will rule the household. This is followed by the *jirtig*, a ceremony in which the couple have a mixture of wood and spices smeared on their heads and beads tied round the wrist and neck. Then they take mouthfuls of milk and blow it over each other as a symbol of fertility.

Some of the converts who marry in Sudan disapprove of this kind of ceremony, considering that it borders on the immoral.

"I wouldn't condone that," says Naimah, talking of the dancing and the scanty clothing. She expects that her daughters will marry in Sudan but plans a very different occasion.

"For a wedding if the bride and groom and the bride's friends want to do something and it's not *haram*, if they're not drinking alcohol and showing their bodies and doing *haram* things, then it's no big deal but it's not something I would want to go to. We have our own idea about what we would like to do at weddings. Our idea is more towards feeding the poor. My daughters and

I see marriage as sacred and I would want them to be more inclined to do things that would bring a good future, bring good *baraka* from Allah for their marriage."

Mikal Mahmoud and Mohammed Abdul Qaadir both had a simple religious ceremony in which a contract is signed at the mosque, followed by a meal for family and friends. This, they believe, is a true Islamic wedding; all the other things are features of Sudanese culture.

Funerals

Like weddings, Sudanese funerals are also frowned upon by some, in this case because of the excessive mourning.

The way in which people scream hysterically, sometimes for hours, to express their grief is a custom which dates from pre–Islamic times. Similar behaviour can be seen on wall carvings on Egyptian tombs. But some Muslims criticise it as questioning the will of God.

Naimah agrees with this. "This is pretty much how I see it. But it's tradition and something that's been done for thousands of years is maybe a difficult habit to break in a short period of time."

Naimah describes the style of Muslim funeral she attended in America.

"We don't do this screaming and crying and moaning in America, there's not this kind of mourning process. The burial process is very expedient. The body is washed, everybody walks the body to the grave where it's going to be buried, there's some *dua'* said and the sheikh will speak to the body and remind them of the questions that are going to be asked of them while they're in the grave. And then everyone will pick up a shovel and start covering the body inside the grave."

In Sudan only the men accompany the body to the grave while the women stay at the house providing hospitality for the many mourners.

"I can understand that," says Naimah. "I wouldn't want to have these women disturbing all the dead people."

Female circumcision

The objections to wedding and funeral customs relate simply to people enjoying themselves or expressing their feelings. A much more serious issue is female circumcision, a practice which can have far–reaching consequences for a woman's health and sexuality.

The practice of female circumcision in Sudan is a classic example of the melding of ancient cultural practice and distorted religious interpretation. Although it is prevalent in a number of non–Islamic African countries, as well as being absent in some Islamic countries, for many people it is perceived as being Islamic.

Female circumcision is a grey area in Islam. There is a belief, though this is by no means unanimous, that it is recommended, but not compulsory, in three of the four main Islamic schools of thought; only one proclaims it mandatory and even then the form prescribed is a minimal, almost symbolic, one. Prophet Mohammed's pronouncement on it was that the cutting should be as little as possible.

Two forms of it are practised in Sudan. In the pharaonic circumcision the clitoris and the labia minora are removed, most of the labia majora are cut away and the remaining parts stitched together to close the vagina, leaving only a small opening. The operation itself causes severe pain and trauma and can cause lasting damage to the woman's gynaecological health. In fact, one of the main causes of Sudan's high maternity mortality rate – over 550 per 100,000 births – is circumcision and its complications. A modified version, the *sunna*, involves cutting away part of the clitoris. In Sudan the pharaonic version is officially illegal although it is still widely practised.

In May 2002 a workshop entitled *Towards the Legalisation of Female Circumcision; Establishment of Training Centers for Operators* was organised by the Ministry of Religious Affairs in collaboration with the Female Student Centre in Omdurman Islamic University. To the dismay of the Sudanese Women's Rights Group, who reported their grave concerns, the workshop recommended legalising female circumcision, raising awareness about its importance in society and supporting the establishment of centres to train practitioners.

Although they themselves must have suffered the distress of circumcision, it is generally the older women in the family who insist on girls being circumcised, so ingrained in them is the idea that without it women are ugly and unclean and unacceptable as wives. Another factor is the belief that in tightening the entrance to the woman's body they increase the husband's pleasure and make it less likely that he will look for an additional wife.

Deirdre remembers hearing of a German wife whose mother–in–law was so horrified when she saw her natural state when she was giving birth that she insisted on her being circumcised on the spot. Deirdre's own mother–in–law suggested that she should be circumcised after having her last child as she didn't want any more.

After giving birth a circumcised woman is normally sewn up again to return her vaginal opening to its previous tightly closed state. Jane Anne described the problems this caused for Su'ad.

"When the lady at the farm had her baby they didn't get all the placenta out and they sewed her right back up. And they sew them so that all that's left is a teeny little hole about the size of the end of your finger. And she hadn't urinated for two days and she was in terrible pain so I said, look, let's get the midwife in and the midwife pressed her around and said there's still some placenta left in there, we're going to have to cut her open again. Well she was just beside herself. She said I'm not going to be cut open again. I said it's not going to hurt you, we're just going to take the stitches out. In the end I had to sit on her while the midwife snipped at the four or five lower stitches. The blood clots couldn't come out because they'd sewn her completely back up again. So she was in absolute agony. So I sat on her while the midwife undid these stitches just to keep her under control. She was screaming and yelling and the midwife slit the stitches open to get the blood clots out to release the urine. And then she weed and weed and weed and weed and weed and all the blood came out and everything and then she felt relieved after that. But of course, she had to get an injection and get it sewn back up again. The reason they sew them is that they believe that the men are going to enjoy themselves but Yazin says that they don't because inside it's still all big and flabby because the baby's just come out so all they do is damage themselves. But this is just the women's belief, you know, that it makes their husband happy, but they don't realise it can kill them. If she'd been in a village and there hadn't been a midwife around she might have died from blood poisoning or something, or an infection."

Jane Anne is not impressed by any religious defence of the practice. "If God is all powerful and he thinks that it's the wrong thing for girls to have pleasure then why did he make them born with it? Why didn't he create them without it?"

Molly, who married into a middle–class family in Khartoum, has not had to worry about the circumcision issue.

"It hasn't come up for us, thank goodness. These days of course, I know it still happens but not as much as it used to, maybe in the villages. You see, in our family it doesn't happen so I've never had to worry or think about that. When I lived over in Bahri I have heard and been very shocked that a neighbour or two will have done that to their girls but it's something that's in very religious, very strict families, but I'd say that ours is a very normal Sudanese family and this sort of thing is not happening. Although my husband's sisters will have all been circumcised they won't be doing it to their children so they've come along in that way."

Mohammed Abdul Qaadir is also spared this problem as female circumcision is not practised in the tribe his wife comes from.

I spoke to Abdel Karim about recent correspondence highlighted in the media in which a sheikh had written to President Bashir to ask for guidance in the matter. The President had replied stating that female circumcision was a recommended Islamic practice.

Abdel Karim drew a clear distinction between the pharaonic circumcision and the *sunna* version. The pharaonic version, he says, comes from an erroneous interpretation. It is based on what Pharaoh did to the women of the children of Israel to ensure their chastity and, although referred to in the Koran as a historical fact, is not recommended in Islam. The *sunna* version – the one approved by President Bashir – is, Abdel Karim claims, to the advantage of the woman as it increases the sensitivity of the clitoris and therefore her sexual pleasure.

"For a man circumcision involves the removal of excess skin around the head of the penis," he explains. "The head of the penis is the centre of the sensitivity of the sexual organ. Likewise Islam also requires that there is the removal of the hood of the clitoris in the case of the woman. This means that the excess skin above the clitoris is removed. Female circumcision as practised by Islam enhances the intimate relationship between a married Muslim man and his wife. It is not, as some people understand it, a way of suppressing sexual desire in the woman. This is totally mistaken."

I'd never heard of this theory and did some searching of the literature on female circumcision. I found first a reference to the removal or splitting of the clitoral hood by doctors in the US, but only as a corrective measure to enhance sexual sensitivity for women who had an existing malformation. The same procedure, oddly, was used in the US until the 1950s to control female sexuality. There was also a Dr Burt in Ohio, known as the Love Surgeon, who promoted what he called "clitoral relocation" (corresponding to *sunna* circumcision) as a means of heightening the woman's pleasure. He operated on women for ten years before being exposed in 1979.

Abdel Karim also objects to the pressure exerted by human rights groups to eradicate the custom. "The UN charter clearly states that the UN does not have a remit to get involved in things which are culturally based. Many years ago the women in Sudan and other parts of the country, be they Muslim or non–Muslim, used to take sharp instruments and cut holes in their faces or make marks on their faces, as tribal marking, and some of them still do. This is not an issue for the UN, although it causes great harm, because the UN states this is a cultural issue. And so is the question of female circumcision whether it is practised correctly or wrongly. And so I believe that these campaigns are totally misplaced and in fact against the UN charter."

Tribal scarring

Abdel Karim's remarks about tribal scarring seemed relevant in the light of what Deirdre had told me about her three sisters–in–law. The story illustrates, as with circumcision, the extent to which people will willingly inflict suffering on themselves and others if they feel it is the culturally correct thing to do.

Their mother had decided that she did not want the girls to have their faces scarred with the tribal marking – three vertical cuts on each cheek – but one day when she was away from the house the local woman who undertook this work caught Amina outside the front gate and did the cutting there and then. When the mother discovered what had been done she refused to pay for it. The woman said she did not want payment, she just wanted Amina to conform to what was right and proper.

Later the two other sisters had it done of their own accord, undergoing a very painful procedure with razors cutting into their cheeks and scissors snipping away at their flesh. But without it they would have felt that they were not the way they should be.

Superstition

Another way in which culture infiltrates religion is through prevailing superstitions.

In Sudan, perhaps more than in most other Muslim countries, there is substantial mingling of superstition with orthodox Islamic belief. Many people believe in spirit possession, *jinn,* and forces of good and evil which affect the lives of humans. They often have recourse to amulets and talismans which they believe will protect them from illness and misfortune. They believe too in the power of holy men to cure disease and bring them good luck.

Zar

The idea of possession by spirits is the basis of a strange and dramatic set of rituals known as *zar,* a ceremony in which women who feel themselves to be distressed in some way by spiritual forces are relieved of their symptoms. These symptoms can be physical – usually psychosomatic – or emotional.

Unlike Christian exorcism ceremonies, the spirits are not induced to leave the person possessed. They are accepted as being more or less permanently attached to the person and need only to be appeased in order to stop their mischief–making. This is done by acting out a set of procedures involving wild music, dancing and histrionic behaviour.

Zar parties have been officially forbidden by the Sudanese government since 1992 but are unofficially tolerated. A Dutch friend who took an interest in these things introduced me to a Sudanese woman who hosted these parties regularly. I arranged to attend one with another friend, Vicki.

Houses in Sudan don't have addresses; streets rarely have names and houses have no numbers. Even when they do, they're likely to be semi–obliterated. Nagla, the hostess, gave me directions over the phone: a list of reference points and lefts and rights and distances. Armed with these we took a taxi and after a few false turns managed to end up at what seemed to be the right place. But something wasn't quite right. As we entered the *hosh* I realised that there was no noise, not a sound, none of the clattering or skirling we had been led to expect of the musical instruments used in a *zar*, not even the chatter of women preparing for the ceremony. We penetrated further and discovered, in one of the warren of rooms surrounding the *hosh*, Nagla and her husband Mustapha, placidly scooping up mouthfuls of *mulah* with handfuls of *asida*.

The *zar* had been postponed until the following day, Nagla told us, and invited us to have some of their lunch. In the usual lackadaisical Sudanese way they hadn't bothered to let us know, but this was a blessing in disguise as it gave us an opportunity to talk with them and get a better understanding of what the *zar* was all about.

The house was a large one, in traditional single storey style with six units of Nagla's extended family living in it, each unit having two rooms and a bit of courtyard. The house was very basic with primitive bathroom and kitchen arrangements. Mustapha, who had a law degree, had some lowly administrative job in a commercial organisation and earned just 20,000 dinars a month (about £42). Yet (in another of these financial contradictions which I came across so often in Sudan) their two children attended a private school.

Nagla told us that her grandmother, who also lived in the house, was a *sheikha*, the name given to a woman with special powers who leads the *zar* ceremony. Her job is to control the proceedings in such a way that the possessing spirits are identified and pacified.

There are a number of different categories of *zar* spirit, Nagla explained. Each type has a different set of songs associated with it; each has its own special clothes and other personal items which the possessed person puts on while the spirit is being pacified. As the song of the possessing spirit is played by the *sheikha* and her band, the affected woman writhes and swoons and acts out her negative feelings, sometimes becoming hysterical in which case the *sheikha* steps in and calms her down.

The spirits are oddly assorted. There are dervishes, Ethiopians and *khawajaat* (foreigners). The group of *sittat* (women) includes Mary the mother of Jesus. The *pashawat* group is for officials from the Turco–Egyptian period.

After we had eaten, Nagla and Mustapha took us to an outhouse where the paraphernalia used for the *zar* was stored. There was an assortment of drums, tambourines and maracas, and a set of gourds, used for producing music by putting them in water and tapping them. Sets of clothes hung from nails on the walls: red gowns for the Ethiopian spirit, a white doctor's cloak for the *khawaja*, a leopard skin patterned shirt for the leopard, an animal skin for the ox. There were spears for warrior spirits and an umbrella for some kind of dervish spirit. There was also a set of whips which some of the spirits liked to use. "This whip," said Mustapha picking one up, "I was playing with it one day and a spirit snatched it out of my hand. He was jealous because the whip belonged to him. He didn't want me to use it. It disappeared, just like that. We didn't see it for three months. Then one night, we were in bed, and the whip came flying in through the window."

The next day we went out again and found the *zar* in full swing in a larger room tucked discreetly away at the back of the compound. The *sheikha*, swathed in a plain red *tobe*, sat in a corner with her group of musicians. We went over to greet her. She had a square face, sharp features and a rather steely look in her eyes. As new arrivals we were each covered with a piece of red cloth. A woman in a mauve *tobe*, cheeks furrowed with three vertical tribal weals, waved an incense brazier under our skirts.

We sat down on the floor with about thirty other women, leaning against peppermint–green walls covered with framed Koranic verses written in elaborate Arabic script. Among them a picture of a rose and a candle with the words *God loves you* underneath stood out incongruously. Under it sat a very fat woman wearing diaphanous green trousers, a tee shirt stretched tightly across large breasts and a long green flimsy tunic. She sat with her legs apart, elbows on thighs, smoking a *sheesha* pipe and staring fixedly with hooded eyes. Despite her ample curves and see–through clothing she radiated masculinity. Popcorn and sweets were passed round. Someone's mobile phone rang to the tune of *I Wish you a Merry Christmas*.

The sheep destined for the *zar* dinner was brought in for a ceremony before being slaughtered. The terrified animal struggled with its handlers, kicked over the incense brazier and defecated on the floor. Someone covered it with the red material and waved the incense brazier around underneath its belly. A group of women walked round it chanting, each carrying a tumbler with a candle and a bunch of leaves in it. One of the women seized its hind legs, lifted them up and marched it out of the room as if pushing a wheelbarrow. The other women followed in conga formation, swaying and chanting and brandishing their tumblers.

The woman for whom the *zar* was being held wore a *jellabiya* of pillar–box red for the Ethiopian spirit. She shimmied around the centre of the room as the *sheikha* rattled her tambourine, singing a harsh, unmelodic song accompanied by three women on drums and another shaking maracas. The woman in red upped the tempo while a woman sitting leaning against the wall started to tremble and cry as if having a fit. The trembling intensified. As she shook and juddered her *tobe* fell off revealing a body–hugging black dress underneath.

A bowl of blood from the slaughtered sheep was brought in and handed to the woman in red. She continued to dance, holding the bowl of blood with arms outstretched. The bowl was then taken from her and passed round the room. As it passed from hand to hand the women dipped their fingers in it and smeared the blood on their faces, on the musical instruments and on their clothes.

More women from the audience were now joining in the dancing. The woman in the tight black dress was alternately hysterical and quiescent. Beside her a woman looking like an Indian squaw in a tan top with leather patches and bits of long woolly fringe was shaking her trunk and her head. A small thin woman crawled on all fours into the centre of the room, thumping the floor rhythmically with her forearms. The women in red pirouetted faster and faster, arms held above her head, and then fell to the ground in convulsions. The *sheikha* stopped singing and crouched down beside her, holding her hand and controlling her movements. The woman in black, now in a kneeling position, was wailing and making frenzied dancing motions with the upper part of her body. The *sheikha* took a handful of salt from a bowl and scattered it over the participants. Throughout it all the faces of three young children outside filled the window frame.

Suddenly the music stopped and all the weird behaviour along with it. People started chatting and passing drinks round as at any normal social gathering.

Vicki and I went out to the courtyard with Nagla where some of the women were preparing the main meal which would be eaten later. One of them had several strings of intestinal tubes in her hands which she was plaiting deftly into a long pigtail. As she did so she squeezed at regular intervals to expel the little brown pellets of excrement still inside. The plaited intestines were to be cooked with the sheep's head – a traditional dish prepared whenever a sheep is slaughtered for a special feast, Nagla told us. Another woman was blowing into something resembling a set of bagpipes. With a tube pressed up against her lips she huffed and puffed. A slithery, crumpled, greyish–pink bag at the other end of the tube gradually inflated. "This is a special delicacy," said Nagla. "The Sudanese like raw lung very much. It will be sliced up and served with liver and stomach. It's easier to slice if you blow it up and it looks nicer." The woman gave a final puff, grasped the slimy windpipe in her fist to stop the air escaping and started slicing.

Ten minutes later the women in the band picked up their

instruments again. The woman previously dressed in red stepped out into the centre of the floor, this time dressed in the clinical white coat of the *khawaja* spirit and smoking a cigarette. She started to dance to a slower rhythm, inhaling deeply on the cigarette, in a trance–like state. The woman in black writhed on the floor like a heap of shuddering black blubber. Nagla joined in. She was dressed like a princess with a bead tiara running through her long black hair, a long magenta skirt and a gauzy silver–edged magenta shawl. As she tossed her head to the rhythm of the band her hair broke loose, flying wild. An old woman, short, skinny and stiff as a ramrod, took to the floor, strutting aggressively. She held two cigarettes between her lips and puffed on them in time to the music. The women at the side made ululating sounds from time to time. The incense was passed round constantly and wafted over all the onlookers.

The body language of the women, especially those who were smoking, was becoming increasingly masculine. They lengthened their stride and swaggered and leered suggestively, though at no one in particular. Samia, the butch–looking woman who had been smoking the *sheesha* got up to take part in the ox dance, stamping heavily and hurling herself backwards against the wall. A woman wearing white trousers with gold gaiters strapped round her calves did likewise.

The music stopped for a second time and everything returned abruptly to normal. A big plastic pail of date juice appeared. It was poured into mugs and handed round. Plates of the raw offal we had seen being prepared followed, garnished with lemon and *shatta* and salt. Vicki and I went with Nagla to her private quarters where Mustapha was lolling on an *angaraib* watching television. Samia, the woman in green, joined us. She seemed to have undergone a personality change, with no trace left of the previous masculine characteristics.

I asked Nagla about the masculine behaviour of the participants. Were they lesbians?

"No," she said. "Most of the *zar* spirits are male and the women are acting like the spirit that possesses them. It's his behaviour."

"And what was wrong with the woman in red?"

"She had a sickness caused by the *zar* spirits. She was sick for a year. She went to many doctors but they couldn't cure her. She went to some sheikhs and they couldn't cure her either. So one of the sheikhs told her to make a *zar* party."

"What kind of illness? What were the symptoms?"

"Her heart beating very fast, shivering, fainting. And she was always feeling that she was going to die. But now after the *zar* she will be better."

"What about the salt that the *sheikha* kept scattering around?" asked Vicki. "What was that for?"

"It's to calm the Ethiopian spirit," said Nagla. "He likes salt. We have to give the spirits the kind of food and drink that they like, and cigarettes if they want."

I asked about the *sheikha*, how she had become a *sheikha*.

"She had a *zar* spirit when she was very young, she had it many times, so she was selected to be a *sheikha*. She was able to treat people, she has the power to control spirits."

The *zar* still had another few hours to go but Vicki and I had to move on. In any case we wanted to avoid the main meal as we were feeling squeamish about the sheep which we had seen being led to the slaughter. We thanked the *sheikha* and said goodbye to the women. They all begged us to come again.

Zar is a controversial issue in Sudan. For some people it is just entertainment, a way for women to enjoy themselves in an uninhibited kind of way. It can also be seen as something much more than that, a much needed safety valve for women to express their frustrations and providing a real therapeutic service. Others disapprove of it strongly as being anti–Islamic. Some are even afraid of what the practice and those involved in it represent.

Although *zar* ceremonies are generally for women only, men can sometimes take part.

Griselda attended one with a male friend.

"I went to a *zar* party in the company of Professor Sergeant of the University of Cambridge. He wanted to see it. There was the *sheikha* and the band but there seemed to be a man, a kind of master of ceremonies, and some musicians. What struck me was that perfectly ordinary members of the public would come in, an ordinary woman in an ordinary *tobe*, and she would sit down and then when this drumming had started and this rhythmic singing and so on, there was a kind of build up of the rhythm and a build up of the excitement and then this woman, who looked perfectly ordinary when she came in, started throwing herself about. Some of the audience were throwing themselves about in an increasingly undignified fashion and their *tobes* were falling off their heads, and some of them were prancing around with cigarettes and one of them was prancing around with a bottle of whisky. In other words it was an occasion for permissive behaviour. And the women would try to do what they heard that the men did somewhere else. I thought it was really quite horrible, actually."

Mikal Mahmoud had spoken of a *sheikha* in his wife's family, a cousin. It seemed to be something the family felt very reticent about.

"She was just the black sheep. I don't think anyone threw her out of their house from what Fatima said. In general it's considered shameful that someone would be involved in this. But the Sudanese say, well, this is still our relative. Fatima was visiting the house with her mother, so obviously, although her mother was afraid, she did want to see her relative.

"Fatima remembers being warned by her mother not go to into this girl's room, so of course they couldn't wait to break into her room and they did. They found it empty. They found it was green with green carpeting, everything was green. It just amazed them to walk into this green room, especially in Sudan. There was nothing Sudanese about this room at all. Green carpeting, and of course, any kind of carpeting at that time would have been strange. And green walls, the walls were painted green, green curtains, everything was green."

This *sheikha* was believed to be inhabited by three spirits. "She definitely had at least three personalities. In one she dressed like a man and she would smoke cigarettes. And in another she definitely dressed like a woman. The third one I think was a different type of man."

Unlike Nagla's grandmother, Mikal's relative was controlled in her work by several men. "The cousin was often away working with one or other of these men. There was always someone else, a man in charge, she was never on her own. She spent a lot of time in Saudi Arabia doing whatever it is that she does. And you know, the way I'm hearing it she really didn't get much benefit from this. She was just used. So she was almost like a prostitute and they were like pimps."

The family believed that the cousin had fallen under the influence of a sheikh as a child and had been manipulated for his ends.

"I think my wife found out from her mother that someone specifically had done something to this child. The problem came in trying to remove it. They brought her to a sheikh so the sheikh took that as his opportunity to get hold of her. He removed what was done but he did it to get possession of her. And it was this sheikh that was responsible for her present condition."

Evil eye

A superstition that is found worldwide, in several of the main religions as well as in different folk cultures, is a belief in the evil eye and its power to harm. This belief is commonly held in Sudan.

When people think they have been the victim of this sort of thing they often go to a religious sheikh to have the problem rectified. Jane Anne described accompanying her mother–in–law to one such sheikh.

"We'd heard about this man in Omdurman. You know, sometimes you're told that somebody's given you the evil eye and that's what makes you ill, or somebody's written something and they're supposed to put it in a hole or something, and, a bit like voodoo, it's supposed to do bad things to you. We went because Yazin's mum felt things were getting on top of her, she was putting on a lot of weight, unsteady on her feet, so she thought someone had given her the evil eye. Other people said that they'd been there and that this sheikh was very good and they felt much better afterwards.

"So we all went and we sat in a circle and we were supposed to keep our eyes closed and he went around reading bits of Koran and different things like that and he said, right, now this will relax you, now I want you to open your eyes and I'll come and read a certain thing to each of you. I didn't believe any of this. I thought this was really stupid but everyone else who was with me really did believe in it. So he said what I'm going to do, before I read to you, I'm going to prick your finger and if it hurts it means I can do something for you and if it doesn't hurt it means everything's all right. So he went round pricking everyone's finger, really hard, you know, with the same needle which I thought was very dangerous because there were other people there, they could have had AIDS or anything. And I noticed he really dug it into everyone, and everyone was saying ow, ow, ow. So he said right, I'm going to read to each of you a little bit and I want you to look at me. When he got to me I was thinking, I just don't believe in what you're doing, Sonny Jim. You can read whatever you like to me but I don't believe you. But everyone else was feeling all dopey. He got to Yazin's mum who really is into this sort of thing, she really believes, and she was really sort of looking at him and she was going whooooo, like this. And the man said, right, everybody stay quiet because this lady has really got a genie inside her and we need to do something about it. And he was sticking a needle in her and he was making her finger all bloody and every time he stuck the needle in he was saying come on, come out, come out, where are you? And she was saying I'm not coming out, I'm not coming out, I'm not coming out. I was getting quite worried about this and I wanted to get up and Yazin was saying no, no, no, stay here, stay here. And this man's digging into her finger and saying if you don't come out I'm going to torture you. And she said said, OK, I'm coming out, I'm going to come out of her mouth. And she was sick, into a bucket. I was absolutely flabbergasted, I just didn't know what was going on. And then he sort of talked to her and she calmed down and she was all right, but she was going wow wow wow, doing all these sorts of noises. He talked to her very slowly and she was all right. And then he went round each of us and he just touched us with a needle and said does that hurt? No. Does that hurt? No. And he went to Yazin's mum and I saw him prick her like this and she said ow and he said yes, you should come back again because I need to work on you even more.

"So the next day Yazin said are you coming back and I said no. For one thing I don't believe in it and another thing it frightened me. So Yazin went back and he watched what the man was doing with everybody. And when he was talking into their eyes he was hypnotising them. That's what it was - hypnosis. And Yazin said that the people he was working with were all women his mum's age who succumbed to things like that very easily. You know, they think that this is the sort of thing that you do when you have a genie in you anyway so it's brought out by hypnosis.

"I think most of these – not the sheikhs, but most of these women who they go to and they do all this reading and they say this is wrong with you and that's wrong with you – as long as it makes the person feel better there's no harm in it. I've been to a couple with Yazin's mum and she was really worried when she went in and she was smiling when she came out. Obviously the woman just picked up on what she was saying and made her feel better by saying what she thought she wanted to hear."

Faith Research Centre

For more information about the overlap between religious and cultural practices Mikal suggested I go to the Faith Research Centre in Khartoum. He wasn't quite sure what it was but had read about it in connection with recent scare stories about sorcery which had been attracting a lot of media attention. Rumours had been going round about a group of sorcerers who were approaching men in the market, shaking their hands or making some other kind of personal contact, such as lending them a comb. As a result of this contact the men's genitals shrivelled up, "melting into their bodies", as they reported. Mass hysteria was breaking out and the Minister of Health himself had to intervene with a broadcast reassurance, telling the public that the supposed victims had all been medically examined and found to be intact.

Before contacting the Centre I did a search on the Internet to see what I could find out about it. All I found were several reports posted by human rights organisations about an incident in 1998 involving a Sudanese Christian from the Nuba Mountains who had been incarcerated there for apostasy. The man, Mekki Kuku, whose parents had been animists, had been converted to Islam while at school and had later switched to Christianity. A neighbour, not seeing him at the mosque, had tipped off the authorities. Defection from Islam being a capital crime under Sudanese law, he was arrested and taken to the Faith Research Centre – described by the human rights organisation Vigilance Sudan as an Islamist indoctrination centre – where he was allegedly tortured and kept in solitary confinement before being transferred to Omdurman prison for trial. At that point the Internet trail ran cold.

It was not a promising start. Nevertheless I went in search of the Faith Research Centre and found it housed in a pale green villa in Amarat, a pleasant part of Khartoum where many NGO people live. The Centre turned out to be primarily a clinic for people with psychosomatic problems or diseases that did not respond well to conventional treatment. In fact, the clientele sounded very similar to the kind of people who went to *zar* parties or to Jane Anne's sheikh.

I spoke with Ilham, a young woman who worked there. She fixed an appointment for me with Professor Tigani Hassan, Director of the Centre and also Professor of Pharmacology at Khartoum University.

A few days later I went back again to meet Professor Tigani. He greeted me warmly, shook my hand, fussed over me to make sure I was quite comfortable, ordered coffee and arranged for photos to be taken of us sitting together, all the time talking volubly in a bustling sort of voice. We ranged over a number of issues relating to Islam and Sudan before homing in on my main area of interest at the Faith Research Centre: the grey areas of cultural/supersititous/religious overlap.

"Supersitition is human," says Professor Tigani. "Muslim or Christian or anything, there is no getting away from it. Every religion in the world has one way or another of superstition." He believes in *jinn*. "I tell you personally I believe there are *jinn*." He understands the kind of pressures that exist in people who seek to relieve them with *zar* but maintains that it is not a good thing. "They do things which are bad like using raw blood and in Islam raw blood is just like faeces. It is *najassa*. They use things which are specifically stipulated in Islam to be unclean. Like menstrual blood and writing some of the Koranic verses with it. You can see the insult. They think the *jinn* will not help them unless they have a conducive environment to come. And the *jinn* do not want an environment where there is cleanliness and prayer and Koran. Of course the *jinn* will not come."

In Professor Tigani's view, in a *zar* it is Satan who is asked to give relief to the person under pressure from the *jinn*. "So one of the conditions is that the environment should be as dirty as possible. So in the end you achieve a good end by using very bad anti–religious methods."

I asked him what a good method of *zar* might be.

"You can't make it good because by itself, by definition, by practice, it's bad. You can't make it good. We don't believe in it at all in Islam because the danger is to utilise unreligious things to achieve your end. The whole institution is wrong. A wise person should think of a substitute to *zar*. But you cannot make honey out of salts, as we say. The *zar* in itself, the way it is designed, the procedures, are in toto against religion."

Professor Tigani told me about the Koranic healing ceremonies they held at the Centre, in which the Koran is read to people suffering from various ailments. He emphasised the importance of belief. "You can't read it to a donkey, or to a dog or to somebody who is not believing in the Koran, it is futile. Come and see for yourself. We have sessions for women on Wednesdays."

So the following Wednesday I went to a Koranic healing session.

Ilham took me upstairs to a square, low–ceilinged room with cream–coloured walls. About twentty women were sitting on several rows of white plastic chairs, waiting for the ceremony to start. Some were wearing the *niqab*, some *tobes*, and some were in ordinary clothes. At the back of the room a woman in a waist–length veil was pedalling vigorously on an exercise bike.

A sheikh arrived, old and grizzled, and straight away launched into a mournful wailing without any preliminary greeting. The women sat with heads bowed and eyes closed. As latecomers arrived the sheikh waved them to seats, brandishing his arms like a traffic policeman without interrupting his singing.

After about twenty minutes another man came in, young and good–looking. The older man left as abruptly as he had come in and his replacement took over. The singing became more tuneful and vigorous.

Throughout the healing a woman in a *niqab* and a green dress had been trembling violently, her hand over her face. Another woman in a thick white satiny head scarf like a nun's veil was seized with intermittent bouts of shaking, throwing her head violently from side to side. A third wept silently.

The singer left as soon as he had finished singing. The women waited for individual consultations with a sheikh.

Afterwards I spoke with Sheikh Mohammed Ali, one of the men in charge of administering the treatments. He explained the clinic system. The patient goes first to an organic doctor and then a psychologist, both of whom write a report which will include details of the recommended praying treatment and information from the honey doctor.

Honey is a very important element of Islamic medicine. Muslims believe its use as a remedy is recommended by Allah himself. Verse 16:68–69 of the Koran reads: "And the Lord inspired the bee, saying: Take your habitations in the mountains and in the trees and in what they erect. Then, eat of all fruits and follow the ways of your Lord made easy (for you). There comes forth from their bellies a drink of varying colour wherein is healing for men. Verily in this is indeed a sign for people who think." The Prophet Mohammed prescribed honey as medication for a variety of problems, particularly stomach ailments. He is reported to have said: Make use of the two remedies: honey and the Koran. Honey is generally recognised as having antimicrobial and antioxidant properties and is effective in the treatment of wounds, infections and burns.

The typical presenting symptoms Sheikh Mohammed described seemed to be primarily psychological or simply relationship problems such as marriage troubles or inability to concentrate. Some were rather weird, such as seeing things while sleeping (but not dreams, he insisted), formation of shapes on the skin, or finding oneself unable to stay at work and having to leave again shortly after arriving at the office.

During the praying treatment patients sometimes speak in foreign languages, he claimed. Sometimes they beat the sheikh, sometimes they struggle. After three or four prayer recitals the symptoms disappear.

I mentioned the behaviour of the three women who had seemed agitated during the Koranic singing. This was due to the devil who sometimes talks through the patient's body, he said.

Sheikh Mohammed took a folder out of his desk drawer and pulled out a notebook filled with jottings. They had been made by an Italian woman writing with her eyes closed and controlled by the devil during a treatment session, he told me. The frenetic scribbling had been produced in response to questions put by the sheikh which the woman was resisting. He pointed to one page covered with the words: "A king will punish me if I give you certain information."

He scrabbled around in the folder again and produced two more sheets of paper, written by another person, covered with English words in capital letters:

THEY WERE SENT NOT BY SHE, THEY ARE 44… I AM NOT AS POWERFUL AS THEY, THEY ARE KINGS, THEY WILL ASK A LOT OF THINGS FROM HER. ANOTHER ME WAS SENT BY SHE! OTHERS A LOT, A LOT, A LOT. LIKE THIS GIRL BECAUSE GOOD PURE MEAT, THEY ARE MASTERS, CHRISTIANS, MUSLIMS, MEN, ERITREAN DRUMS…. A LOT, BIG THESE PEOPLE.

"Who wrote this?" I asked.

"One girl, I think African. Devil say through her tongue."

"Was this during a Koranic reading?"

"Yes, he speak through her tongue. We know she can't speak English, but in this time she speak English. After prayer she can't."

He handed me a newspaper article in Arabic which told the story of a woman who had gone into a bathroom. Her sister removed the light bulb, said Sheikh Mohammed, whereupon the devil entered her body.

"When she came out she couldn't see. The devil entered her body. How do we know that? Certain thing happen in her body. She couldn't see in front of her. When we pray in front of her, devil speak to us. He said that he saw her in the bathroom and entered her body and he will go out after an hour. And after an hour devil disappear. And after that this girl can see completely."

"How did you make the devil go away?"

"Through prayer. And an organic doctor said that is a strange kind of disease, not organic. There is a certain kind of partition in front of her and we say the devil made this partition. When we prayed, this partition disappeared. After that she became well. This is a kind of infection of the devil."

Sheikh Mohammed dived into his drawer again and extracted an X–ray. He laid it on the desk and pointed to a number of whitish lines. "Here are needles," he said. "In all parts of the patient's body. But after praying treatment the needles all move to one part of the body. So it is easy for the doctor to cut open and remove the needles."

"How did the needles get into the person's body?" I asked.

"Through magic," said Sheikh Mohammed.

7 DAY TO DAY

Integrating into a different culture involves an enormous amount of practical adjustment. The converts in Sudan were embracing not only a new religion but also a new way of life affecting everything from the food they put in their stomachs to the clothes they put on their backs, from the treatment they got when they were ill to the education they could provide for their children.

Sudanese food

One of the most distinguishing features of a country is often its cuisine but there is nothing in Sudan to compare with the couscous of North Africa, the pasta dishes of Italy, the smorgasbord of Sweden, the curries of India.

Many foreigners find Sudanese food unappetising. Meat and fish are plentiful for those who can afford it but there is not much variety in their preparation. The range of fruit and vegetables available is limited, especially in summer. The local staples are: *asida*, a stodgy porridge made from sorghum; *kisra*, a sour–tasting pancake–like bread; *ful*, an oily brown mush whose principal ingredient is Egyptian beans; and *tamia*, deep–fried balls made of ground chickpeas. There is usually a dish of *shatta* on the table, a spicy red chilli sauce.

As with the pig in China, no part of the sheep is ever wasted in Sudan. As well as the lung and intestine dishes I had seen at the *zar*, there are recipes for the hoofs and the head. The hoofs, after being skinned, washed in a flour–water paste, and cooked with onions, garlic, spices and sometimes carrots, produce a nutritious gelatinous soup. The head can be boiled with onions, and the tongue and the brains fried.

Molly's family have always kept to a mixed diet. When she first came to Sudan she lived in her husband's family house and she and her in–laws shared their food.

"In my flat I would cook more of the food that I would like, more British food, and I would take them some. I would take down some of my soup or chicken or whatever and then when Mubarak would come in from work he would bring up the *mulah*, the Sudanese stew. It worked out quite well, I would give them some of my dishes and they would give me some of theirs."

Molly now lives in her own house where she has a staff which she has to feed.

"I've always done my own cooking. I've never had someone cook, but now that we've moved we have to feed the workers and you wouldn't be able to afford to feed them on our sort of food every day so I now have to have a cook who will cook the local Sudanese stews. There are a few things I would know but not as well as they would do it and not really well because I don't like it as much. They eat traditionally, you know, *khudra*, it looks like a spinach stew, almost like a slime. It's very healthy, it's full of iron. That takes many hours. That's the problem. A lot of their food takes a long time to cook. They have to cut up the leaves like you would herbs with that curved knife. It takes ages to do that to start with and then they'll add some meat to it but I don't know how to cook it because I don't like to eat it.

"A lot of the workers, they wouldn't be given so much meat to eat. Like today she'll be making a sweet potato stew. In the summer they'll be eating more things like *molochia*, which is a spinach–type stew or the potato or sweet potato stews, or okra. Aubergines too are used a lot, aubergine stews. In the winter it's much better. Then we do get the cauliflower and the cabbages coming so you can vary it a bit. But it's expensive. It would more be the likes of us that would be buying these really. The poorer people here probably have a healthier diet. The richer ones will probably be eating too much meat. The poorer ones will probably be concentrating on the vegetable stews. And the *ful*, of course, which is the main dish."

Zarina is in an unusual social position in Sudan as a single woman living independently, working in Khartoum and living some distance from the city in a rented room. She eats a lot of snacks, fast food and takeaways.

"I eat *ful* but *ful* isn't my favourite dish. I like *asida* and *tegalia* which is minced meat with red sauce, and *asida*, that floury porridge stuff, and you can have the *tegalia* around the *asida* and eat it with a spoon because it burns your fingers, or you can have one that they mix with yoghurt and eat that with *asida*. Then bring me the *abreh*, that drink they drink in Ramadan, it's lovely. You've got white *abreh* which is good for thirst management and red *abreh* which I like to break the fast with."

The Sudanese normally have only a drink of tea or coffee early in the morning. The full breakfast is much later, lunch is eaten mid–afternoon and dinner late evening.

"For breakfast, at about ten or eleven I eat bread and anything I can find," says Zarina. "Like if I'm at work I tend to just buy anything I can get my hands on: *ful* or *tamia* or minced meat or cheese, and Maza, that's mango juice, the thick creamy one. Sometimes I'll have a hot dog or a burger. I don't have lunch usually, maybe some dates or Sudanese peanuts mixed with sultanas. In the evening I have supper at about seven, eight or nine. When I go to the Central restaurant in Souk Arabi I have bread, *tamia* and egg sandwich with mango juice. Their cafeteria is not very clean and it's very busy, it's like Victoria train station. I go to the rough one. Sometimes I go to a chicken place. The place is too small and too dirty and packed, but the food is good. I sometimes buy *halawiyaat* which is Arab cakes with the many crunchy layers and almonds in between."

Jane Anne took to Sudanese food like a duck to water.

"I loved it straight away. I liked the spices and the flavour of it and the way it was cooked."

She also likes the way in which Sudanese people eat, without cutlery and all gathered round communal dishes on a single tray.

"When I first arrived from England I got into the house and because my father–in–law had been in England a lot he knew how people had their lives in England. He knew that for breakfast you had jam and cheese and different things like that and bread – he even found sliced bread, by the way, which you didn't get very often here – and they'd set it all out on the table with the knives and the forks and the plates and a big pot of tea with the cups and everything, just like a normal British breakfast. And they said: would this be comfortable for you, is this the way you want to eat? And I said, well, you know, I'm going to live here for the rest of my life. I knew that Yazin sometimes used to eat with bread and, whatever we were eating, he would put the knives and forks aside and use the bread to soak it up. So I said if I'm going to live here I might as well live like that. So they cleared the whole table off and they brought a *sinnea* – a *sinnea*'s a big round tray, it's like a communal eating thing – put the cheese and the jam and everything on plates on the *sinnea* and put the bread around the side, and then we cooked a big omelette and then I think she'd done some meat and some chicken and things, and we all ate together like that. And that's the way that I've carried on eating although a lot of foreigners here won't. And it's much easier for them now because they find whatever they want. You can even find Marmite and things. You can find anything you want here. But when I first came you couldn't. You had to search around for things. If you were desperate to have cornflakes you'd have to go and search for it. Aisha said she wanted cornflakes and we went out a couple of times searching, then after that I said: no, Aisha, you're not going to have it. You're living in Sudan, you eat the Sudanese food. She pulled a few faces but she was fine after a couple of days."

Health

Another thing that poses a problem for foreigners is the standard of medical care.

Sudanese hospitals have long had a bad reputation, not just with foreigners but with the Sudanese themselves. Most of those who can afford it will choose to go outside the country for treatment. The nursing standards are particularly low. "They just don't seem to care," says Jane Anne. "And there's no follow–up. You know, you might have an operation but the nurses don't care about you after, so you die after the operation."

I spent ten days in hospital in Sudan, laid low by a viral illness. Although it was considered the best hospital in Khartoum at the time, the level of hygiene made it likely that you would leave more ill than when you arrived. Every day a cleaner came into my room carrying a yoghurt pot with a toilet brush in it. She used the brush to scour the toilet pan, down into the bend, up under the rim, and then carried on using the same brush to pretty up the washbasin and polish the taps before going off to do the same thing with the same brush in the other rooms. For the blood tests I needed the technician couldn't get his needle into a vein and kept stabbing at my arm till the crook of my elbow resembled a pincushion. I fainted. When I came round the man refused to make any further attempts, saying he felt too nervous.

Lena had her second child by caesarian section in the same hospital.

"I guess I said, OK I survived, but it was very difficult. The very next day, six hours after the operation you have to stand up so they can give you a bath. And the next day I was out going home. We were on the third floor and we wanted to take the elevator and of course in Sudan you've got all kinds of problems that face you. The elevator was broken, and it was a Friday, so I had to walk down three flights of stairs after a caesarian. And I was holding my stomach and moaning with every step that I took."

Three weeks later Lena developed DVT in her leg. She went to a different hospital for treatment. In Sudan patients are expected to have at least one family member with them when they go into hospital to do the general kind of looking–after tasks that would normally be done by nurses. Lena didn't have this kind of help as she had no family members in Sudan.

"I had a newborn baby beside me in the bed and I was sick and I had an intravenous injection (IV) in my arm and I had to change his diaper myself and had to fix his bottles myself. I was in the hospital and trying to take care of the baby so no wonder with all the moving all the blood was going back up in the IV. Then the baby kicked it out."

She felt that the nurses were not properly trained and that they learned 'on the job'.

"It's not that they come in having the knowledge, they're just plain practising with you. It was midnight and they were trying to put a new IV into another place and it was two nurses working together and they couldn't find a vein, they couldn't figure out where to put it, they were poking me in the arm about five times, five tries that failed and hurt, and she was trying to force it into my hand. I thought she'd destroyed the nerve in my hand. It was blue for two weeks after that."

Fiona, a British nurse, had a hair–raising experience at her husband's niece's wedding a few years ago when one of the guests fired a pistol to signal the signing of the marriage contract. This is a traditional custom which is now illegal but is still common. The bullet hit one of the other guests, passing through the abdomen from right to left with such force that it broke up inside him, leaving three exit holes. The first hospital he was taken to refused to let him in as any admission involving a criminal matter has to be reported to a government hospital. At the second, with Fiona trying to staunch the flow of blood, there was an argument between two doctors about the treatment to be given. The family finally piled the patient on to a trolley and took him to another hospital round the corner where he was operated on. They all donated blood but it was still not sufficient and he had to be given untested blood from the bank.

Mikal Mahmoud has had more positive experiences and he has no worries about his children being medically disadvantaged because they are in Sudan rather than the US.

"I think because of the overall environment it's much healthier for them to be here, especially living out in Soba. The diseases that they do pick up, the medicine or any necessary treatment they may need is available."

He was impressed with the medical care given to his small daughter when she had an accident with hot tea and suffered second degree burns. She was treated with the traditional Islamic remedy, honey.

"It was a freak accident, the adults weren't paying attention, someone put the teapot on the ground, maybe she grabbed it, maybe someone kicked it, I don't know. She was severely burned. My wife immediately picked her daughter up and threw her into a barrel of water. Of course, everyone else was going crazy thinking my wife was trying to drown her. But finally after that we took her out and took her to the emergency ward. It was a severe second degree, but it was only treated with honey. And it was excellent treatment."

As well as the Islamic remedies, there are a lot of traditional tribal practices.

Deirdre's husband remembers having mumps as a boy and being taken to an abandoned house where mould from the walls was rubbed on his face. Eye complaints were sometimes treated by making incisions on the face, lung complaints with incisions on the chest. Pleasanter remedies included milk with dates soaked in it overnight or with a heated stone dropped into it to be drunk by patients with a fever.

Jane Anne described a process similar to the branding of cattle which is believed to cure jaundice and to build up the strength generally.

"The two little boys on the farm weren't eating very well and they were very weak and they burnt them in a line all down their backs with a metal prong which they put in the fire. They believed that it would make the children stronger and make them eat better. And just after that one of them was very ill and went into the hospital to have a drip. He'd lost a lot of fluid and the doctor was having a look all over him and he asked about the burns and the mother said, 'Oh this is because he hasn't been eating very well and it's to make him strong.' And the doctor said, 'Do you realise this might be the reason he's actually ill in the first place? You know, it might be the shock from you doing this.' This is just certain beliefs of certain tribes and you can't stop them. It all boils down to that. The way they're brought up."

Jane Anne's mother–in–law was born when her mother was still only 13. She had become pregnant before even having her first period. Molly's mother–in–law was born while her mother stood with her arms tied to a tree, a traditional method used to enlist the help of gravity in the birthing process. "But nowadays things are very modern and deliveries here are quite similar to those in England," Molly says. "If you've got money, you can even get epidurals now."

After delivery in Sudan the mother is supposed to stay in bed resting for forty days. These forty days can be exhausting as she will be receiving a constant flow of visitors.

"We had thousands of people in the house all day long for weeks after I had each of the children," Jane Anne recalls. "I had to put up with people coming in, people coming out, saying congratulations and everything. It was very tiring."

Beauty care

As well as playing hostess after giving birth the mother has to maintain her physical appearance which means spending hours on the application of henna, a paste made from plant leaves and used to paint the skin. Many Sudanese women like to have their hands and feet patterned with henna all the time but for important occasions, such as births and weddings, it is mandatory.

"Whenever I had my babies, when the nine months was ending I put henna on specially," says Jane Anne, "because people come and see you in the hospital as soon as you've had it. It's a nice thing, it's a traditional thing, and all of the women normally have henna on when they have their babies. And then you also do it before the seventh day which is the naming day. It takes hours to sit down and put it on, and then you have to sit for about two hours afterwards for it to take and then you have to sit on the *dukhan* which is a hole in the floor which you put coal and sandalwood in which makes the henna darker. But on white people it also makes your skin darker so for a foreigner sometimes it makes them look a bit silly because not all of you goes the dark colour. You know, if you're leaning on yourself you have lines across your arms and legs, and you have to keep putting your head in so that your face goes a little bit brown otherwise you have this brownness up to here and then your face is white. So I do that on special occasions but I won't do it if, like at the moment, I'm so busy with the house and the farm and there's no particular wedding that's coming up in the family or anything like that."

Traditionally a bride's beauty preparations start long before the wedding. Unlike the West where a suntanned skin is supposed to be attractive, Sudanese women prize a lighter shade and they sometimes go to great lengths to change their skin colour. In the past a Sudanese bride was not allowed to leave the house for several months before the wedding so that she could be fattened up and kept out of the sun. At the same time she treated her skin with face masks made of custard or potatoes and other concoctions and exfoliated herself with *dilka*, smoked balls of sorghum mixed with powdered sandalwood. She would also use the *dukhan* intensively, to the extent that the surface skin could be peeled off, revealing a shiny new one underneath. Usually, even now, all body hair, except on the head and the eyebrows, is removed with *halwa*, a sticky sugary substance which is applied to the skin in strips and then ripped off. Another custom, one which is dying out now, is the practice of tattooing the lips shortly before marriage. The lips are stabbed with a thorn and kohl, or sometimes crocodile urine, is then applied to give a blue–black colour.

Clothes

Looking nice is not just for special occasions. A smart appearance is important to the Sudanese and they take great care with their clothes. Zarina found to her surprise that the Sudanese were shocked at the casual way foreigners dress. "They used to ask me why the *hawajas* go dirty and I said because the place is sandy and they don't want to dirty their clothes so they just wear some old trousers and tops. And they said yes, but we live in the sand and we go clean. Some of them took it as an insult, some of them wondered why, is it their culture to go dirty? After that I started looking at my clothes."

The traditional male dress for Northerners consists of a long white robe, usually worn over white trousers, with the billowing folds of a white *emma*, or turban, encasing the head like a baked Alaska. If he wants to look very smart, a man will also have a loose white scarf with grey stripes at the ends draped round his neck. When dressed up like this older men often carry a walking stick. Businessmen and professionals generally wear shirt and trousers during the day at work but often change into traditional dress in the evening. Many others wear *jellabiyas* all the time, and may be bare headed or with an embroidered skullcap instead of the *emma*.

The short *jellabiyas* of the *Ansar al Sunna* comply with instructions laid down in the Koran and the *hadith* where it is stated that clothes should reach mid–calf, or at most the ankle bone; any longer is a sign of vanity or pride and abhorrent to

God. Some of the less strict Muslims mock the *jellabiyas* of the *Ansar al Sunna*, claiming that they are kept short to avoid being defiled by trailing on the ground in the pit toilets. For this reason the *Ansar al Sunna* have been given the nickname *Abu Hamman*, Father of the Toilet.

Mikal generally wears a loose grey cotton outfit of baggy trousers and tunic reaching down to mid–calf, closer to the Pakistani style of dress than to the Sudanese. He often has an embroidered hat of some sort perched on his head. Mohammed Abdul Qaadir has adopted the Sudanese *jellabiya*. Male converts generally dress in one of these two ways, or simply shirt and trousers.

Women's dress is more varied. Younger women mostly wear ankle–length skirts, long–sleeved blouses and veils which range from thick waist–length coverings fastened tightly under the chin to light and lacy strips of material covering only part of the head. Many married women wear the *tobe* over their other clothes, a long piece of material wrapped round the body rather like an Indian sari except that it also covers the head. Although it is possible to hide the hair completely with a *tobe*, the more devout women also wear a close–fitting cap underneath.

It is rare to see a foreign woman wearing a *tobe*. "Everyone wore them when I came in the early 70s," says Deirdre. "I found them a hassle as they slip and you need to keep adjusting them. Now even Sudanese use safety pins but not in the past. Now they are less common as the Islamic dress is easier to wear, and less expensive."

The dress of Muslim women contrasts with that of the many Southerners in Khartoum who are free to wear whatever clothes they like, although they are on the whole quite modest. Tall, slim, ebony women from the Dinka, the Nuer, the Shilluk, the Azande and many other tribes, often in flamboyant African tie–dye dress, stand out like birds of paradise.

Foreign female converts have never been subject to the dress code enforced by the Public Order Police and many of them don't wear the *hijab*.

For Molly it's something that she's just not used to. "I rarely go out but if I do go out I make sure my arms and my legs are covered. It really is just that last bit of getting the headscarf on."

Jane Anne doesn't normally wear one but she feels that it is part of the culture and is appropriate for certain occasions. "If I go to a wedding or a funeral or something I wear one as well. If I didn't everyone there would look at me as if to say: Oh, why are you not wearing one? And it looks quite nice. I do it in the mirror, make sure it looks nice, and off I go."

Education

A big issue for people moving to a new country is the education of their children. This is particularly true in Sudan where the majority of children are educated in ill–equipped schools, in classes of sixty, seventy or more, often with text books shared between four or five other pupils or even no text books at all. The teachers are often untrained, sometimes with little knowledge of the subject they are teaching.

Many Sudanese, despite their low incomes, have their children educated in private schools though the standards, particularly in terms of premises, furniture and facilities, are usually quite low. This is reflected in the fees which are often only about $100–$200 a year.

Mikal's children go to a private school. He pays 60,000 dinars a year for each of them (about $230).

"There are about thirty kids in a class and they get new text books and they have some computers but by Western standards it's quite primitive. But they get double the amount of Koran that kids in government schools get."

Abdel Karim, who has the advantage of having two wives who are teachers, home–schools his children. "I'm very disappointed about the level of schooling in Sudan. I believe that schooling at an early age, it is essential that it is done correctly in order that children grow up with an understanding of their religion and themselves that is whole and complete."

He runs his school along the lines of a *khalwa*, an Islamic school which focuses on teaching the Koran. For this he has the help of a teacher who has memorised the Koran. Other children join in during the holidays.

At the other end of the scale there are two international–type schools, one American and the other British–based, with large numbers of expatriate teachers. As well as this, a number of small private English–medium schools are beginning to appear, staffed mainly by Sudanese teachers and whatever native English speakers the management can rope in locally.

Jane Anne is critical of the educational system but she has never considered sending her children to the international schools where most of her friends' children go.

"There are too many kids to a classroom. And the teachers don't pay enough attention to the kids and they always have a ruler or a piece of stick or something and they're not frightened of hitting the kids. All of my friends' kids go to Unity or the American school or one of the sort of more higher schools but when I came here I said my kids are going to be Sudanese, they're going to go to a Sudanese school. They're going to be brought up in the Sudanese way."

Social mores

Being brought up in the Sudanese way is much more than a question of schooling. It involves imbibing the whole ethos of a society which is community–focused and prizes respect for others. One of the traditions underpinning social life in Sudan is that of *nafeer*, a system of mutual support. In the past this translated into people helping each other to build their houses, harvest their crops and so on, with the host providing food for the helpers. It is still seen today in the way people rally round with help for weddings and funerals which are major social events, with dozens or even hundreds of guests to be catered for. Women send food round on trays or in an *amoud* (a pillared container) to supplement what has been cooked in the homes of the deceased or the bridal couple, or they will give sums of money to help defray the expenses. These are not gifts so much as loans, with the recipient being expected to reciprocate at a future occasion, and there is always someone recording the money given, so that the recipient knows who gave what.

Much of the social life in Sudan revolves around these occasions and the obligation to attend funerals, marriages and naming days is strong even when the people concerned are only remotely acquainted. Deirdre commented on the amazing memories the women had, particularly those who were not educated. "They could remember exactly who did or did not come to pay condolences or proffer congratulations at events going back decades."

An expatriate Sudanese may spend a considerable part of a holiday back home visiting all the houses that have had a death, birth or marriage in their absence.

"This is particularly strong outside the capital," says Deirdre, whose in–laws live in a village. "On the first opportunity, a personal visit is expected. Even sending a letter, or nowadays an email, is not sufficient."

Closely related to this is the principle of *beiti beitak*, 'my house is your house' which lies at the heart of Sudanese hospitality. Visitors may drop in at any time, family members may come to stay unannounced, and the hosts must put themselves, their houses and their belongings at their disposal. Deirdre found it difficult to get used to this invasion of her privacy. "I don't like people helping themselves to my clothes or hair–brush, or looking in cupboards or into my handbag. But the 'my house is your house' gets taken to extremes. No one can understand if I get upset if something of sentimental value is broken or 'stolen'. I suppose they are realistic, and our richer society has given us the materialistic attitude and sense of ownership."

The principle of respect for others contributes to making Khartoum a relatively safe place in terms of personal security. Compared with most other capital cities it has very few burglaries or muggings, though there is some evidence that this is beginning to change as rising standards of living create more temptation. In 2003 there were reports of people cruising around in cars, stopping foreigners to ask for change and then snatching their purses.

Prostitution was on the increase too, with women simply hanging around in certain streets as if waiting for a lift and then getting into cars with clients. The women were often university students driven to this to make ends meet. My neighbour, Abdel Gadir, was a gynaecologist and full of lurid tales of illegitimate pregnancies, abortions gone wrong and sexual infections.

On the whole though, Khartoum is still a place where the converts feel comfortable about bringing up their children.

"I think I'm happy that my children are brought up here," says Molly, "although you'd be surprised at how much of the West has come into Sudan now with the satellite. They're up with the latest of everything that's going on in the West but I feel that they're safer here. You know in England you'd worry about kids even going out to play in the street. You don't feel that here."

Jane Anne shares this view.

"I feel so much safer here for my kids. You can go out at night and you don't have to worry about being beaten or raped or kidnapped or something. All the things that you see on the English television, it's no wonder that girls get pregnant before they're married and people being raped and things like that because they show it on the television. When I went to see my dad before he died, I walked in and he was asleep, so I turned the television on and it was children's hour and the presenter had this mini–skirt and a vest top on and you could see everything and I said, God, it's no wonder that the kids don't know how to dress and people get raped and things like that. I was just talking to myself and my dad said: Go back to Sudan, will you."

Mohammed Abdul Qaadir is not so comfortable with the behavioural standards in Khartoum. He feels that Islamic principles are no longer properly observed and is not happy about exposing his wife to many situations of daily life because of the mingling of men and women.

"For example, I feel very uncomfortable when I have to ride on public transport with my wife in that men and women sit next to each other. The scene is very crowded and very tight. When it's time for everybody to go home, everybody stampedes the bus. I can't have my wife doing that. And not only that, you'll find that when a man gets on a bus and he sits next to a woman, they don't acknowledge that this is a Muslim woman, I'm a Muslim man, there should be some separation between us. They sit next to each other, touching each other. For some people it's their way of flirting sometimes. I can't stand for that. Most of the buses here in Khartoum come from China and they're not appropriate here in Sudan. So generally I tend to rent a private car if I go someplace with my wife and I don't allow her to walk in the *suk* and things like this because the Islamic etiquettes of relationships between men and women have been lost in Sudan."

Another Islamic ideal which seems to have been lost in Sudan is that of racial equality.

In her writings Lena refers to the "community of belief" of all nations and races and people who follow Islam. "The only religion that has strived so hard for the equality of humankind has been Islam. Islam does not recognise race, nationality, gender, social class, tribalism, etc. All humans are equal and deserve respect and dignity."

The Sudanese population comprises a wide–ranging ethnic mix. Many of the people in the North are products of intermarriage over the centuries between the indigenous inhabitants and Arab traders and settlers. The flow of pilgrims from West African countries travelling to Mecca and often settling in Sudan added to this mélange. Even in the Christian/Animist South, which has remained on the whole black African, there is a diversity of tribes. Physical types vary throughout the country from light brown Arab appearance to coal black.

In his Farewell Sermon, Prophet Mohammed said that he placed tribalism under his feet. He called for unity and just treatment for everyone, no matter his race, gender, nationality or social class. He stated: "An Arab is not better than a non–Arab and a non–Arab is not better than an Arab. They are equal like the teeth of a comb." According to the Koran: Allah judges only people's hearts and all people are equal except in their level of piety.

Despite this, racism is rife in Sudan. Northerners often look down on Southerners and non–Arab Westerners. The many Southerners and Westerners who live in Khartoum are disadvantaged compared with their Northern counterparts. They are the ones who do the menial work and the labouring jobs, and who form the enormous domestic infrastructure of servants, cooks, drivers, dhobis, guards. An amazing number of Northern families have at least one such person helping in the house, provided with some basic lodging and paid a pittance. Even Sudanese standards of physical attractiveness are based on the idea that the lighter the skin the more beautiful the person.

I wondered how African–American converts felt about being part of a racist society. Naimah in particular had complained about discrimination in America. Was her decision to live in Sudan not implicitly condoning racist attitudes?

"It's almost like, it's nothing unusual because in America you have a light–skinned African–American, you have a dark–skinned African–American, and the light–skinned African–American thinks of him or herself as a privileged caste and looks down on the dark–skinned. So that's something that is in the nature of mankind, I'm better than he or she because...

"Believe me, the same kinds of attitudes are imposed on the African–American anywhere. That's life, and it's our test. And the same for the African who is looked down upon here. It's their test. And also it's a test for those who are looking down upon them because the day they look down, tomorrow they'll have to be looking up. It's a test, everyone's being tested."

8 CONVERSION – THE REASONS WHY

People convert to Islam for a variety of reasons. The attraction of the Muslim way of life with its emphasis on family and social values can be just as important as doctrinal beliefs. In a survey of Muslim converts carried out in the early 90s, American researcher Joseph Smith reported that the majority cited social reasons as their primary motive for converting. These reasons included the comprehensive nature of Islamic social laws which provide a complete guide to life; the greater discipline enforced by Islam which makes it more effective than Christianity in dealing with social ills; the level of personal safety and the low crime rates found in Muslim societies; the protection of women; the provision of a sound moral and religious education for children.

All the converts who speak in this book were previously Christians of one kind or another. The step from one monotheistic religion to another is not such a big one and for many Christians Islam offers a satisfactory alternative to a creed in which many of the tenets require too great a leap of faith.

Four out of the five converts whose stories are featured in the following pages are black. This ratio is not representative either of conversion generally or of the relative numbers of converts in Sudan, although it is true that proportionately more blacks than whites convert to Islam in the West. More than half of the converts that I knew of living in Sudan were white.

The Nation of Islam

For many African–American converts their first introduction to Islam is through the Nation of Islam.

The Nation of Islam, also known as the Black Muslims, evolved out of various black nationalist organisations in the United Sates. The movement proper was set up in Detroit in the 1930s by a black door–to–door salesman, Wallace Fard Mohammed, who claimed he had had a vision from Allah giving him a message for black Americans

Fard vanished mysteriously in 1934 and was succeeded by Elijah Poole who changed his name to Elijah Mohammed and claimed to be the "messenger of Allah".

Under Elijah Mohammed the movement enforced rigorous obedience to a strict behavioural code based on that of Islam and emphasising hard work, piety and accountability. It promoted the social power of black communities and was successful in improving the lives of blacks in drug–ridden urban areas. Its aspirations, with their implicit promise of restoring dignity to an abused and subjugated people, appealed strongly to many of the deprived and disillusioned migrants from the South living in the black ghettos of the northern industrial cities.

The Nation of Islam diverged in many ways from orthodox Islam and was more of a black separatist and social protest movement. Its creed included the claim that Wallace Fard Mohammed was an incarnation of Allah, the doctrine of black racial superiority and the teaching that the white race was the result of a genetic mutation engineered by an evil scientist, Mr Yacub, 6,000 years ago.

When Elijah Mohammed died in 1975 he was succeeded by his son, Warith Deen Mohammed, who started to make radical changes. Over the next decade he did away with all notions of black racial superiority and the deification of Wallace Fard, aligned the religious practices with that of orthodox Islam, and renamed the organisation the American Muslim Mission.

In the meantime, a splinter group which adhered to the original beliefs and the separatist social vision broke away under the leadership of Louis Farrakhan. This constitutes the Nation of Islam as it is today.

Malcolm X

Another influential figure in attracting African–Americans to Islam was Malcolm X who joined the Nation of Islam while in prison in the 1940s. He rose to prominence in the movement, becoming its most effective speaker and proselytiser. A dedicated supporter of black pride and black self–dependence, he had, as a child, seen his house burned down by the Ku Klux Klan, his father murdered and his mother committed to a mental institution. Conflict within the hierarchy led to his suspension from the Nation and in 1964 he renounced his views about black separatism and converted to orthodox Islam. He was assassinated in 1965.

Mikal and Mohammed were actively seeking a more credible and spiritually satisfying religion when they came to Islam. Both mentioned the Nation of Islam as figuring along their route but, like many African–Americans who were attracted to it as a social movement, they did not feel that it was the true Islam, or even truly a religion.

"It was a black nationalist group who used a lot of Islamic terminology," says Mikal who became involved in their social programme. "When I saw the theology of the group I knew this was not the truth, but I told them I'd help them build their nation. So I worked for them."

But he became disillusioned even with their secular activities.

"It turned out that basically they were a bunch of crooks, ex–cons and gangsters, ex–ministers of churches; these were the black people that were running the Nation of Islam. It was quite a scam. But for several years it worked."

Mohammed was aware of the Nation of Islam from an early age as he spent part of his childhood in Detroit where it was founded. Like Mikal, he was impressed with their social programmes but not their religious ideas.

"Although they were somewhat appealing I never considered them as a group that I might want to belong to. They were incorrect in their beliefs about the races, about white and black, about things like that."

He was more influenced by Malcolm X.

"I was looking for something more spiritual, something that would allow me to attain a higher state. So after reading Malcolm X, which opened my eyes to what was happening around me in Detroit, because Malcolm X spent a great amount of time in Detroit, I was able to try to ask myself: what is the purpose of life and why did Allah create mankind? And what is my purpose in life exactly? What am I going to do in my life and how am I going to do it? I wanted to realise that it's important to contribute to the community and give back to it what you have benefited from it."

Naimah joined the Nation of Islam in the late 1960s. Already a practising Baptist she started to become interested in Islam when she was studying comparative religion at college.

"When Islam came to me it was like, wow, the direct words and emphasis on God being one and there being no other god and no other entity like Allah. That was very striking. I had no problem with Christianity but the more I learned about Islam, the more I grew bothered about Christianity's emphasis on the trinity. I was really grabbed by the way the Islamic chapters in our school book described Allah. I loved that description of Allah but at that time I was in school, I was raising children. So I said I'd wait a while."

Later a chance invitation to a Nation of Islam event won her over on the spot and she remained with it until 1975, the time when Warith Deen took over.

"In 1975 Elijah Mohammed died and I began to study the

Koran on my own. There were a lot of things drawing Muslims to study the Koran at that time. Even his son, Warith Deen, was encouraging the Muslims to study the Koran. So doing that, not only did they begin to realise the truth of Islam, the true practice of Islam, but also the nature of what the Islamic movement inside the Nation of Islam was about personally, spiritually."

For Naimah the Nation of Islam was 'the door that she had to walk through to get to the door of Islam'.

A problem that comes up constantly with converts from Christianity is the doctrine of the Trinity, which holds that the Godhead is a threefold figure comprising the Father, the Son and the Holy Ghost. How, they ask, can Christianity be monotheistic if the deity is made up of three persons? To this mathematical conundrum is added the inequality in status of the three personalities. God the Father seems to be the one who rules the roost, Jesus Christ is subservient to him, and the Holy Ghost is a kind of walk–on part making fleeting appearances as tongues of flame on the heads of the Apostles or as a dove. Another common stumbling block is the idea that Jesus, the man, was also God. How can a being be both human and divine? These were the two things that made Molly decide that Islam offered a more intellectually satisfying creed than Christianity.

"It was the problem I had with the Trinity, and also the problem of Jesus being God. Even as a child of five I would pray to God and then I would pray to Jesus. I always separated them. I'd had this belief since I was very small that God was one, even being a Catholic, so it was like, it answered my questions of when I was a child."

Lena also had problems with the Trinity

"I was trying to be a devout Christian before. I was very active in the church and the choir and reading the Bible every day. I wanted to be close to God, but I couldn't figure out what I needed to do to be close to God. And the church, they kept saying to ask in the son's name. So I tried to ask in the son's name, and I didn't feel comfortable with it and I went back just to praying to God. I could not logically see how three could be one or how God could have a son. It seemed like Roman and Greek mythology to me."

Her journey to Islam was catalysed by an affinity she discovered for the Arab culture.

"I started meeting Arabs at the university and having contact with Muslims but they were not practising Muslims. But I did learn about the culture, which attracted me. I was attracted to the food and the language and I wanted to know more and I kept bothering them. They kept mentioning every now and then Islam, especially because Ramadan was coming and they fasted in Ramadan. And of course they brought me some books in English about the basic beliefs and the pillars of Islam and I started reading them. And then I bought a translation of the Koran in English and I read that. I was reading and trying to hide it from my room–mate because her father was a minister. I would read late at night after she slept. Then I met an American Muslim who was wearing *hijab* and I took my *shahadatan* with her. She asked me why I wanted to become a Muslim, I told her because it's the truth and there's only one God and Jesus is a Prophet and Mohammed is a well respected Prophet also and that this made logical sense."

For Zarina the attraction was first of all social and cultural. As a child she was influenced by her peer group at school, the majority of whom were Asian.

"When I was little I was always more attracted to Islam because of the people doing things together and having a beautiful and mystical culture and something everlasting, ancient and beautiful."

As an adult this attraction was reinforced by her perception of Islamic communities as more supportive and accepting than Western ones.

Griselda too spoke primarily of a social motivation, the desire for greater integration with her Sudanese family.

"It was something that I had been contemplating for some time. My parents had died and there was nobody in England who was going to be upset by me changing from the Christian religion to the Islamic religion, and having lost so many members of my own family I was more and more integrating into my husband's family over the years. And I thought, well, I want to be more integrated with them. I want to be totally acceptable to them and be part of them and live and die with them and be buried with them and so that was it. And of course my husband was overjoyed but he had never ever pressed me himself. So it was a happy thing."

Any fears she may have had about not being found sufficiently knowledgeable were dispelled by the experience of a friend who was about to get married to a Sudanese woman.

"My young friend Patrice, when he married he was told that he'd got to convert to Islam so he went to a Sudanese *sharia* judge and said I want to convert to Islam now. And this judge said to him: do you want to convert to Islam because you believe in it or because you want to marry a Sudanese young lady? And he said: because I want to marry a Sudanese young lady. And still the judge converted him. So I thought well it's not going to be such a big ordeal, I'm not going to be put through a first–class examination and put to the test. It seems to be quite easy."

Griselda also told the story of a German friend.

"She went to visit the Mygoma baby home and this baby in the first ward kept clinging to her. And so when she went round she asked the director to go back to the first ward and she did and this baby again was clinging to her and she picked him up from his cot. The director said to her, you can take him if you like because they're only going to die in here. And she just took him, spontaneously, just like that and went walking out of the gates. And as she got past the gate this director called after her and said, oh by the way you are a Muslim aren't you? And she said oh yes, yes, yes, yes. And she wasn't but she went and converted to Islam the next day, out of love for this child that she'd just picked up. I thought that that was a wonderful story. I met her husband on the Haj the next year, and he was wearing his *ihram* and sitting on top of this travelling bus and singing praises of the Prophet. I said: *Mabruk*, Sigrid's converted to Islam. He said: She only did it because of that baby. And I said to him: But whatever way it comes about, what a good thing to happen. I thought this was a wonderful story that this woman had just like that converted to Islam out of love for that foundling baby."

9 MIKAL MAHMOUD

Mikal Mahmoud, a burly figure with a bushy, greying beard, has been living, working and praying in Sudan for twelve years. His personal philosophy is summed up in the first line of his CV where he states his objectives: to live a peaceful life, to die a Muslim and (concluding with a typical roguishness) to make a few bucks and babies on the way. So far he has made four babies and he makes dinars rather than bucks; he has no desire to cross swords with anyone and has remained steadfast in his chosen faith for nearly thirty years.

His story begins in early 1950s America.

I was born on 10 July 1952 in Los Angeles, California, the fourth of eleven children, seven boys and four girls. I was born Michael Stephen Murphy. Catholic family, Catholic upbringing. When I was 5 we moved to Pasadena and I did all of my primary school at a Catholic school in Pasadena followed by high school at Don Bosco Insitute in Rosemead. After high school I went on to study English, first at California State University followed by UCLA in Los Angeles.

It was a very typical, somewhat conservative, black Catholic family upbringing where my parents, who both worked for the Los Angeles Board of Education, saw fit to have our upbringing basically in the hands of the priests and the nuns. They sent us off to school and that was our upbringing. Home was more just general chores and homework. Every year we took about a one month vacation and there were also family outings scattered throughout the year. Religion was something simply understood;

we were Catholic, this was our religion, this is what we do and we did it. As a child I was happy with my life and religion was part of it. I accepted it unquestioningly.

In retrospect I'd have to say my parents were very religious, but at that time we saw it as just normal. My father belonged, I think, to two church organisations. My mother didn't belong to any organisation but she supported every activity that we were asked to participate in. They sent a letter saying we want the children to do this, she persuaded us to do it. I never got into deep philosophical discussions with my mother on religion. I found out later that she was more liberal in her viewpoint towards others in terms of religion. She had no problem with me becoming a Muslim. My father seemed to be a bit stricter but again he didn't like to talk about religion

I can't put a finger on any time when I began to question Catholicism *per se*, or Christianity, or religion. At high school I had broadened to the concept that Christians are Christians. It wasn't a question of Catholics are right and all other Christians are wrong. That concept was definitely gone by high school. But sometime between graduation from high school and dropping out of university I had doubts, clear doubts, as to the validity specifically of Catholicism but generally of Christianity and any other religion that I happened to come across. But I did believe in God, I did believe there was a God and he was the Supreme Being and I just accepted that I don't really know this God, who he is, and he's going to have to tell me. I was looking at Buddhism and Hinduism and other Eastern religions. One thing I do remember is a certain acid trip where I kind of had a conversation with God where I came to the conclusion after coming down from the acid that all the religious people that I had known up to that time were liars. They were saying things that were not true and I did not know why. I had no answer for why these people were lying. It was in the acid experience that these questions arose, it was as if I was having a conversation with God. Who are you? Why are these people doing this? This type of thing. And the answers were: 'I don't know' type of answer. So like I say, when I came down it was kind of replaying this experience. Probably not talking to God, I was talking to myself. I kind of rationalised it that way. So I resolved at that point that my mind would be open in terms of my search for God, that my tests as to whether whatever I happened to find was true or not would be stringent, there would have to be clear proof.

Mikal dropped out of university after two years, feeling that his life there didn't have any direction.

After I dropped out of the university I moved to San Francisco and when I arrived there, I found some people involved with a group called the Nation of Islam. This was my first exposure to anything called Islam. I had just heard of them but never really had any knowledge of what they were really about and I was given one of their newspapers. The thing that attracted me to this newspaper I was reading was that this was the only newspaper that I'd seen in the US that was taking a position in support of the Palestinian people and it was quite surprising. So I said I want to know more about the group, not about the religion but about the group. And this is when I found that they had a programme to build a black nation; that black people must do for themselves, this type of language. And having been a dropout and having nothing better to do, I said OK, I'll help you build your nation, and I joined them. They had a number of little business ventures and I ran a fast–food joint for them. It was interesting. A lot of people used to come by and tell me their problems. I was sort of like a father confessor. But it was almost like slavery. The pay was almost nothing, whenever I got it, and the living conditions were quite poor. But I didn't care because this was an experiment. I wanted to see where this was going to lead. It was a challenge. The fast–food joint was my only involvement with them. I didn't go to the marches or anything or to the temple.

*Unlike many blacks growing up in America in the 50s and 60s,
Mikal was not aware of any racial prejudice.*

I was naïve, I didn't realise till later what it was. Our neighbourhood
was mixed – black, Mexican, Japanese, white. And my high
school, Don Bosco, was for smart kids, competition was high,
racist attitudes were irrelevant.

It's true that one of the key civil rights cases sprang from
Pasadena, and the Black Panthers from California, but the situation
in California was nothing like in the South. California was one big
party. This was just one of the themes. Black rights, gay rights,
Jewish rights. Everything was a party in California. Everyone was
participating in everyone else's rights. We called it 'movement'.
We'd say: What's happening this week? Oh, the Jews. Let's go.
Nowhere in any of these movements did you find Islam.

*Neither was Mikal motivated by a strong feeling of identity with his
ethnic background.*

I knew I was black but I wasn't a slave of black culture. I mixed
with everyone. At the university I was exposed to many Jews.
I had a lot of Jewish friends. I didn't think I had to *act* black
to prove that I was black but this challenge of building a black
nation was simply a challenge that I saw. It amazed me that these
people could have this challenge.

Then I met, inside the movement, another guy – he was older
than I was – and he, interestingly enough, had been what you
might call orthodox Muslim. I found out later it was not a true
orthodox movement he belonged to but it was closer to Islam
than the Nation. And he had left that movement to join the Nation
of Islam. For basically the same reasons as I did, just basically
wanted to help build the nation. He was kind of getting tired
of this other group. And he began to explain to me that there
is a religion called Islam like this and like that. So I went back
to my old quest: let's start testing this religion. And this religion

answered all my questions. I questioned it for about a year and a half. After a year and a half I was absolutely convinced, this had passed all the tests, the basic questions of theology. Who is God, what are we doing here, life after death. I wasn't so much concerned about ritual or things like that. I was looking for the essence.

Allah is the Supreme Being, he is the creator of all creation, he created man as proof of his ability to create. The story we find in the Koran is that there are angels and there are *jinn* and he said I will create man and they said, no, you shouldn't create man, he's not like us, he will kill, he will disobey you, and God's response was: I know, you know not. One of the things that convinced me about Islam was that man is perfect in Islam. But he's given the permission to do as he wishes, to leave his perfection. And the way to remain in perfection is by following the guidance of Allah.

If you take not only Christianity but Hinduism and Buddhism, all of them have the concept that man is not perfect. Christianity has the concept that man is filth and he was cleansed by the murder of Jesus for all of us and all we have to do is to accept Jesus and accept being cleansed and then we can go and do whatever we want to do after that. We are saved. Which made absolutely no sense at all. Whereas the Hindu and Buddhist and those types of religion say that man is not perfect but that he can move towards this perfection through various deeds and kind of discover his path.

We returned to the question of the proof that Mikal mentioned earlier.

If a person were to read the Koran, the Koran defines who is God and it defines who is man and what is his purpose in life and what is his relation to God, all of these theological questions. So it got down to either this is true or not. And the Koran doesn't just leave it up to raw faith as to whether you believe in this or not. It challenges doubters and it challenges doubters in more than one way. First it asks the question; Is this a book from man or is it a book from other than man, meaning a supreme being, meaning God? If this book is from man then let man write another book equal to the Koran. I didn't quite understand that challenge. So this is one reason it took time for me to accept it. To understand the challenge you have to have at least a basic knowledge of Arabic and Arabic writing to understand that no Arab could live up to this challenge till now. No Arab could say, yes, man could write that Arabic book. Once I saw that I accepted at least partially that part of the answer. Further when one looks at the history of Prophet Mohammed we can see that he had to receive information from somewhere and there was no proof that human beings provided him with the information that he received, that we find in the Koran. Many scientific statements are made in the Koran that man did not develop till hundreds of years later. This was further proof that the Koran was true and it was from God. I think those were the areas that helped convince me. First, I came to the conclusion that either the Koran was true or it was not true. If it's true then it answers all of the questions that need to be answered, and proof of its truth lies in the Koran itself.

One of the five pillars of Islam – the five duties incumbent upon a Muslim – is the Haj, the journey to Mecca. Mikal made his pilgrimage while he was still living in America.

It just happened. The opportunity came to me like that and I snapped it. The desire was there but I really didn't see a way, I didn't see how I had the money. The opportunity just came. I met a man who said he was making the Haj. I said how are you making the Haj, because he had about as much money as I did, and he mentioned a mosque where he had gone and there were apparently some people who had paid for their tickets and couldn't go and they were offering their tickets to others; I went there, talked to the man in charge and he asked me if I had a passport. I said yes. He said OK. He asked that I do small work for him, messenger work, shuttling passports between the mosque and the Saudi consulate. And during the Haj he asked me to be someone mildly in charge of the new converts, this type of thing. He knew I could speak a little Arabic. So I did, and that was it.

Did this play a part in my decision to come to Sudan? Well it would be hard to say no, it had nothing to do with it. Islam teaches that whatever you ask for while making the circumambulation in Mecca you will receive. I asked for three things. I asked for a good wife, I asked for the ability to speak Arabic and I asked that I not be the only one in my family that would be a Muslim. I didn't get the wife till I got here; right before I left one of my brothers converted to Islam; and I came here to learn Arabic. You have to understand, I tried to learn Arabic in the United States and I came to the conclusion that I was never going to grasp the language as long as I stayed in the United States just taking lessons, that I had to go to an Arabic speaking country. So in that sense yes, I was convinced that I was going to learn Arabic and seeing that I wasn't learning it in the United States.... But if the question, to ask it with a different emphasis, is: did the Haj direct me to Sudan *per se*, only Allah knew that my wife was going to be from here. I had no idea that I was going to get married in Sudan.

Adopting the moral and social codes of Islam created no conflict for Mikal, nor was he subject to prejudice on that account.

In America my social life revolved around neighbours, family, old friends, weddings, birthday parties. I was still quite independent. I didn't join any Muslim groups so this gave me a lot of freedom. I didn't have a lot of peer pressure in that sense. At the same time because I didn't join any Muslim groups I associated with almost all... So in terms of the non–Muslims, you know, I didn't really see it as part of my agenda to convert anyone. I was a Muslim, they didn't want to be Muslims, this was quite OK with me. We were working together, we were socialising together, I don't drink, I don't smoke. If you can live with that....

I won't say that there wasn't any prejudice but again it was still California. In California, you do your thing, so if your thing is being Muslim, people let you do it. In fact, you can say this is maybe one of the problems I've had with the Muslims. Whether they were blacks, or Mexicans or Arabs, they were bringing the old prejudices that they had into Islam and you know, they were saying, OK, you don't like me because I'm a Muslim whereas before they used to say you don't like me because I'm black. And I didn't have that growing up – 'you don't like me because I'm black'. This was simply not something imposed on me. If it happened, as I say, I didn't see it.

When I left America it was only to study Arabic. I did not leave with the intention of never going back. What actually happened was that I got here and looked back. This is when I saw America. It's like being in Los Angeles on a smoggy day. You don't notice it until you leave and then you get up on the mountain and you're looking down on top of the smog and you say – I was breathing that! And you say – I won't go back into that. This is how I feel about America. When I got out of America and went to the *Merkaz Islami* here in Khartoum all of a sudden things that I had read before, I thought – hey, I see what this means now. All of a sudden things had more meaning. When I looked back at America I saw two things: I saw that in that American environment I would never get this insight. It's being here that has given me this insight that I have. The other thing that I saw was that what I had thought was some sort of fringe Islamic life – that we were not living in America because you simply can't do it – coming here and living it I realised that no, this *is* the Islamic life, it's a part of Islam to live this life and if you go back to America you won't be able to do it. That's what made me decide that I wanted to stay in Sudan. Maybe go back to visit in America but that's all.

Mikal studied Arabic for two years at the Merkez Islami (now the African University) in Khartoum.

I was living on the campus, in the dorm. I was 39 at the time. The other students were mostly Nigerians, Ethiopians, Somalis, some from West African countries. All Muslims. Everything was paid by the university. I entered without any money. They fed you, they gave you soap to bathe, a bed, sheets, mattress. It was funded by the Gulf States. We were four to a room. We had the toilet and showers at the end. There were about three tiers. A lot like an American prison. The food? Food was food. Having worked as a cook for nine years, food was food. Just something to stop me being hungry. Things like food, things like dress, living conditions had no meaning. You know, I had seen so many different extremes. UCLA is in a very well–off area of LA. So off campus was life among the rich and famous. I cooked in Malibu, well–known hangout for rich people. I met a lot of rich and famous people. You get invited to a party, you meet the sons of rich and famous people. This is what I had gone through in my life so rich people meant nothing to me, famous people meant nothing to me. This type of food, that type of food, this type of clothing, that type of clothing, this type of car, that type of car, all of that lost what it might mean for other people. I don't care. Which makes it quite easy for me to live in Sudan. I can accept it.

While still living in America Mikal had become involved with an organisation called Jamaa' Tabligh, a missionary movement set up by Sheik Muhammad Ilyas Kandahlawi in India in the nineteenth century. Their key principles include the need to adopt a simple lifestyle and an obligation on the part of followers to go out into the wider Islamic community to spread their doctrines by teaching, and good example. Mikal continued to work with them in Sudan.

In the US they are the group that are best known for practising just rudimentary actions, practising fundamental Islam. Dressing exactly this way, walking exactly this way. Every single aspect of life, every action, they define it in terms of how you do it in fundamental Islam and they teach people how to do things this way. It's all like a form of exercise, and what they do is they go around from mosque to mosque and ask people to go with them for a period of time – a weekend, three days, seven days, ten days, thirty days etc. and during this time they teach all these different rudimentary things. It's kind of like Amway. Amway is a multi–level marketing scheme in the US. I mean, it has no end. I mean you go out and you get people and you tell them, come with us and they come with you and you say go out, go get people to come with us and they come with you and it's just like this. It's almost a joke among the Muslims that these guys, where are they all going? If they just want to show me how to eat, how to dress, well, OK. But they call me and they tell me to come, and then they ask me to tell other people to come and it's this Amway–type activity.

Of course, anyone who's serious about being a Muslim is attracted to the concept of learning more about his religion, about things that he's doing wrong, about things that he should be doing. This is attractive. And when people first meet them they're quite attracted to them and they want to join them and they want to do things.

Of course, the conflict in America is that you have to eat, you have to make money, and so people don't have time. In America I never would sacrifice more than a weekend. Also they put on a lot of pressure, especially when they see that someone is slightly attracted to them, they try to pressure him to come join them. One way I got out of the pressure in the States is that I said to them: listen, I'm going to go to Sudan and I'm going to go out forty days with your people in Sudan. So when I came here I said to them, I'll help you out for forty days and I did.

So I joined up with these people. About half were Sudanese,

the other half Egyptians, Pakistanis, Indians. We spent one week in Khartoum, went to about three different mosques, and then we spent thirty days in the west of Sudan. The main town was called Um Ruwaba. But we only spent about half the time in Um Ruwaba itself, the other half of the time we went out into the villages. We were treated like very special guests. Of course, their lives are very simple. They just eat a type of porridge called *asida* with *weka* poured over it (dried okra pounded into a powder and you make a soup out of it) three times a day. There was one village where they were a bit better off. They slaughtered a baby goat, other places they slaughtered a chicken. The houses were just little grass huts. Not even mud. In fact, if you saw mud it was a sign of the existence of ample water, that they could use the water to make a mud house. Mostly we slept on the ground without going inside at all which is kind of the normal way of living in Sudan. You go inside just to get some shade. You can get shade without walls. Sometimes people sleep under a *rakuba*, which is the same grass material over your head but no walls. The mosque itself might not have a roof, might just have a low wall.

It was an eye–opening experience for me coming straight from the US, straight from Los Angeles into the deserts of Western Sudan. People were living in the middle of nowhere, from one nowhere to another nowhere. And they're surviving, finding water. In one village they used to give the kids these jerrycans and they'd ride out, for about forty–five minutes on donkeys and they'd come back filled up with water. Where they got it I don't know. But every morning we had tea; with milk. In this area watermelons grow wild. Now these aren't the watermelons that we have here, with the red meat inside and you slice them. These watermelons are kind of green inside, and they're full of water, and they take them and store them, and throughout the year they could break them open and use them for refreshment when there's no water. They had chickens and the chickens would find their own food and eat the rind from the watermelons. They had goats and the goats would provide them with milk and provide them with meat.

And during the rainy season they farmed – tomatoes and okra and this type of stuff that they can dry and use for the rest of the year and what's left they can sell in Um Ruwaba.

The thing was just to go around from village to village and try to get the people to pray, to follow the religion as it's supposed to be followed. About three days in each village. I was like the attraction. It was like a travelling circus. I was like the three–faced woman.

To go into the villages we split into groups of about ten. We would come into a village and then at the first sunset prayer they would stand up and announce who they were and then they would say that they had an American who had accepted Islam; he's going to talk about Islam. Then I would say some things and they would translate and then after that they took over and talked to people about the importance of practising Islam and that they needed to spend some time with them to kind of rejuvenate themselves. But the real thing, the real objective was to get people to travel with them. This was actually the thing. So after the third day they would say, who's going to come and travel with us and how many days are you going to come.

So usually by the third day we would have a band of men or young boys, teenagers, ready to come out with us and then we'd move the next village and do it all over again. We were about ten, but we would move in a group of about twenty or thirty people and of course they would fall off from village to village. They would go back home.

Normally from village to village we went on foot. We would leave a village and you would reach a point at which you can't see the next village and you can't see the village that you left. That didn't last long. You would go on and then about ten minutes later you would start to see the next village.

In one of these villages something happened that really touched me. I saw a little boy who was walking without any shoes. So I asked him where are your shoes (meaning kind of plastic sandals). He said another boy took them. So we said, go get them back from the boy. He said: I asked him to give them back and he refused and the reason he took my shoes is that his were old and broken and mine were new. So we said why don't you go to the man in charge and tell him so that he can straighten this problem out. The little boy said, I did. So we asked him what happened and he said, I was told to bring the boy before him and I did. So we were all at that point very, very interested in how this thing was going to end. So we said, what happened. He said that the older man told them both to swear to God that the shoes belonged to them and that God would decide the situation. And we said, yes, this is a proper way to solve the situation. Normally no one would tell such a lie. Normally the one that was stealing the sandals would have enough fear. So we said, what happened. He said, the other boy started to swear to God but I stopped him. I said take them. We looked at this boy and we said why did you do that? The shoes belonged to you. He said yes, but if he had sworn he would go to hell. I didn't want him to go to hell for my shoes. This touched me. It made me think again about Sudan. Wow, Sudan is a good place.

Soon after that Mikal parted company with the Jamaa' Tabligh.

I had to challenge them because they're quite forceful. When I was studying at the African University they used to come by and ask why they hadn't seen me for so long. So I promised that I would pay them a visit and I paid them a visit and I saw them recruiting and heavily putting pressure on young people to go out with them. So I just challenged one of them. Why are you forcing people to go out with you, making them feel bad if they don't go out with you? Where in Islam does it say that we have to go out with you? What is your objective? And I told them, I'm sorry. I'm a Muslim. I call people to Islam, I don't call people to go out with you. I told them no, there's more to life than that. There's more to Islam than that. And so we parted company. Now I don't belong to any group, any association. In the Koran it says, hold on to the rope of Allah and don't break up into groups.

It was through the Jamaa' Tabligh that Mikal met the man who was to arrange his marriage.

While I was going out with the Tabligh I met a Sudanese who had spent some time in America. So I hung out with him while we were doing this. When we came back to Khartoum his brother or cousin had an office and I went to that office as kind of a meeting place. And I met the accountant for this business. We had lunch, we talked. I didn't see this man for maybe five or six months. He lived at the time in Dubai or Abu Dhabi or somewhere in the Gulf. He came back to Sudan to do some work for this man in his office, saw me and just mentioned: Mikal, I hear you're looking for a wife. And to cut a long story short, he said: There's a girl in Kassala, I'll set things up and he did.

He went there with my picture, showed my picture to her and she tentatively accepted. He came back and said OK. I got on a bus with him, we went to Kassala together. I met her. I met her on a Friday and we were married on Monday. It was a very simple wedding. In fact, Monday was a delayed time. There was a flood that lasted a day. A seasonal river broke through the place and flooded the area and we spent all Sunday sandbagging to keep water out of the yard of the house. By Monday morning the water had gone down so we went out and bought a sheep and some extra food. That afternoon we held the marriage contract. At night a few of her friends came by and did the singing stuff they do and that was it. She stayed in Kassala and I came back. For one year I would simply go visit her.

Mikal's stipulations for what he wanted in a wife were modest.

Just that she was a Muslim, that she was not looking for money. I wanted it to be made plain that I had no money. So that was plain and they accepted it under these conditions and I married her. I can get along with anyone as long as they can get along with me.

Before I met my wife I only went to see one other. And when I saw the attitude of the people, all the money that they wanted, I was just so fed up. I'm not going through this, I said. I don't know how I'm going to get married but I'm not going through this again. I'm not going to knock on these doors and talk to these people.

Mikal had been married and then divorced in America. Had his ideas about the romantic aspect of marriage changed since then?

I knew that love was something that would come later. I believe that you don't love someone till you know them, you don't know them till you live with them so if you think you love someone and that's why you marry them, what's going to happen when you find out later that you don't love them? I married my first wife because she was single, she was available, she seemed like a good person – at that time meaning she came to the mosque. That was a good Muslim to me at that time. Any woman that comes here is good. I fell in love with her after we got married. We had a strong relationship. But as I and she went in different directions my love could not overcome my desire for Islam. And she honestly thought that I could be a Muslim and we could still have this relationship. She didn't understand why I couldn't go to the mosque with my Muslim friends and have that lifestyle while she at the same time could go and have a different lifestyle and at night we go home together as husband and wife.

Mikal had not planned on settling down in Sudan immediately, even after getting married.

I had clear plans that I wanted to go back to America, I wanted to work and then come back to Sudan. One of the things I wanted to do going back to America was get some kind of wind turbine, a windmill or something, for pumping water, for Sudan. I knew nothing about the technology, but when I went out with these missionaries and we were way out in the west of Sudan I was taken to this village and I saw that they needed water and actually the borehole had been drilled in the past, there was just no way to get the water up. And they were taking great pains to protect this borehole. I thought, these things in California, these wind turbines, that's what they need. I'll go back to America, bring one back for this village. I met another American here. He had already determined that wind energy was a solution for Sudan and he had intentions of building some wind turbines. So when I met him and I saw all the information he'd brought with him I thought hey, there's no need for me to go back to America to bring the wind turbine. You're here and you're ready to go. I'll help you. So at that point I decided that there was no need for me to go back to America and I unfortunately gave a lot of attention to helping this man and he turned out to be a bit off. (*Laughs*)

So that didn't come to anything. Anyway I was married at that time and then some other things happened. And through all that my wife and I had come to the realisation that it was probably best that I not go back to America, that I stay here and make a life out of this, and my mother agreed and my father also agreed. I wouldn't say they were happy but they said, you're in Sudan and you're gonna stay in Sudan, OK. They sent help, they sent some money. They visited.

Salaries and standards of living in Sudan are very low. Most people, by Western standards, are poor. There is no stratum of society which corresponds more than loosely to Western notions of a middle class. How does Mikal adjust to this?

It's a different system here in Sudan for sure. In the US you live off your credit card and you work with the idea of making payments, you kind of budget everything out because you can buy with your credit card, you can do business with the credit card as well.

Everything is centred economically round the American credit system. Here in Sudan everything is centred more round the family, your relatives, who you know. So I found it quite difficult to get involved economically in Sudan. Also my wife's family is very poor so rather than being able to look to them for some assistance, if I have anything in excess I'm going to probably have to use it to help them out.

But this is what makes it so nice because I am here for Islam. I am here because I want to be a Muslim. I want to practise my religion and so, whereas in America it's quite easy to depend on your credit card, without that credit card and without all these things I have to depend on Allah and that's what I'm forced to do. So I have to accept the Islamic economic system which is that you don't provide anything for yourself no matter how hard you work, no matter how much you sell, no matter what. All provision comes from Allah. So work and work hard and do your best and then thank Allah for what he gives you.

Mikal and his family, and usually one or two members of his wife's family – a brother or a cousin – live in Soba Hilla, an outer suburb of Khartoum.

When the British left, a few families took over the farmland here in Soba which at that time was far enough out for the government not to pay any attention. And they established themselves there so the people there now, the older people, are the second generation. Now it's definitely a suburb of Khartoum, everything is moving in that direction, it's starting to become quite developed.

Converting to a new religion and moving to another country involves big changes in one's lifestyle. I wondered if it had been accompanied by any changes in Mikal's character and personality. If he had remained in the States would he have been very different from the person he is now?

I don't know if I should say – unfortunately not *(laughs)*. I can't get away from myself. I thought that being me would get in the way of things in Sudan but I find the Sudanese are quite tolerant. I'm still the same old me. I admit that Mikal as a person, the Mikal that existed in the US, I don't see how that Mikal fits in Sudan. But he does. I don't have to apologise for being me but I know that I am this African–American Californian *(laughs)* in the middle of this third world African country and I am reminded almost daily that this is the situation but I guess the Sudanese are very tolerant people.

10 FATIMA

I asked Mikal if I could talk with his wife, Fatima. I'd hesitated, fearing he might think it an intrusion.

"Well, there's a problem," he said slowly.

He's going to refuse, I thought.

"Who's going to translate?" he asked, beginning to grin.

"You."

"Oh, no. I should keep out of this."

"Well, Rianne then," I suggested, naming a Dutch friend who spoke fluent Arabic.

The grin spread.

"Hey, you know, that would be really nice."

Rianne and I took the bus out of Khartoum, down the Medani road where clusters of sheep up for sale nibbled their last meal, past the Haj Centre, a magnificent domed building like a palace or a top of the range mosque where pilgrims book their trips to Mecca, beyond the Soba Aradi displaced camp lying off in the distance, through stretches of semi–desert wasteland littered with rubbish, to the outlying suburb of Soba Hilla. There was a lot of building going on in Soba Hilla: piles of bricks and other building materials everywhere, mounds of earth, trenches and holes for the laying of pipes. The tarred road was still under construction.

At Mikal's house a young man opened the gate and took us through the courtyard, past a goat pen, and into a narrow room with an earthen floor and unpainted mud walls. There was a door to an inner room where a fan swished over a sleeping 8–month–old baby.

I had met Fatima once before, at Abu Bakr's *yom as samaaya*. There, dressed in a thick green outfit like a nun's habit, she had seemed stout and ponderous. She walked in now, slim and lithe, in a loose long shift and with her head uncovered.

"*Salaam aleykum.*"

"*Wa aleykum salaam.*"

We shook hands and made introductions.

Fatima went to the kitchen to fetch some colas. An older man, Fatima's father, came in and shook hands with us.

We sat on *angaraibs* and chatted about this and that, about Kassala (her home town) and Khartoum, about her children. She had fine features and a kind of aristocratic tilt to her head. She supplemented her words with frequent expressive hand gestures.

We wanted to know what it was like for her, with her traditional Sudanese upbringing, to be married to an American. She joked at first saying that she had never been married to a Sudanese so she didn't really know. Then she continued:

"The difference lies in giving up not just the Sudanese customs but also the American traditions. The difference if I was married to a Sudanese is that we would have lived according to the Sudanese customs but with Mikal, we married according to Islam, we live according to the religion. We see what is wrong, what is *haram* and what is *halal*. So we live according to this. So we did not marry according to traditional Sudanese customs and we are not doing the American tradition. We follow the religion.

"Of course, Mikal is more committed to the tradition of Islam than I am because he is a convert. He became a Muslim by his own will, and I am a Muslim by tradition, because my mother was a Muslim and my father and so on. When you become a Muslim by your own choice you know much better what Islam means and he knows much better because he has studied what right Islam is. For example, my father, he shook hands with you. In the right Islam this is not OK. New converts to Islam are far more strict and they follow the right Islam."

Her decision to wear the *niqab* is her own choice and is not imposed by Mikal.

"The *hijab*, you have to wear the *hijab*. You see in Sudan a lot of women are not wearing the *hijab* but only a scarf. The *niqab*, some people say you have to wear it but I say although it's better it's not really necessary. In the beginning it was not comfortable because in Sudan it's hot but you get used to it and then you feel good with it and when you go out without the *niqab* you feel as if you're going out naked. My friend Samia when she came from America she said it's so difficult here, the dust, the hot wind, the hot air, the heat. She was allergic, so the first two or three years were very difficult and then she got used to it. So everything when you get used to it, it just becomes normal."

Socially there are differences for Fatima in being married to an American.

"There are not as many visitors as in a Sudanese family. It doesn't matter to me. When there are a lot of guests, it's OK, when there are not a lot of guests it's OK too. The difference is when Mikal has guests coming it's organised, so we know that somebody's coming tomorrow, for example, it goes by appointment. It's not like the Sudanese way where you can just pop in and expect anybody to pop in at any time. We know that somebody is coming. So in this way it's not Sudanese. But people from my side, my family members or whatever, they just come in without an appointment."

Fatima had felt a bit nervous about marrying Mikal.

"I was scared because it was very strange. I was hesitating but of course, with us you don't refuse your father. When he tells you to marry you do it. The only thing I myself wanted to do was to study. I wanted to finish secondary school. It was not a big problem the first year in Kassala but then we came to Khartoum and I became pregnant so it was difficult. Only after Mustapha was born could I finish secondary school. So I have a Sudanese secondary school certificate and I would love to go on studying at the university and Mikal says you can, you can study at the university, it is no problem but the problem is practically – because of the children, if they get ill, it's difficult to go out.

"Before I married I wanted to study law but now, at the moment,

I just want to learn. I want to study and it doesn't matter what I study. I'm interested in a lot of things. It could be languages or Islamic law, anything.

Talking of America Fatima says: "I just want to see with my own eyes what America looks like. I hear a lot of people talking about it and I just want to see it with my own eyes, just for once. I don't want to stay there, just to see. Mikal doesn't want us to go to America now because the children are too young. When the children grow up they will know much better what is wrong and what is good. Now they might be influenced."

The girls have unusual names: Mearaj, Malafdh and Munjida. Fatima laughed as we tried to work out how to spell the names in English letters.

"Mikal names the boys and I name the girls. This is not really normal in Sudan but this is what we agreed upon. Mikal wants a boy to have a good firm name like Mustapha or Muhammad or Ahmed but for the girls I choose a name and I like to choose a beautiful name, a special name, maybe a little bit cute name, because it's the only thing a girl has, her name. Because her name is her name and it is connected with her life. A boy, his name will go on because he will be the father of a son or a grandfather so his name will go on but a girl, she'll take the name of her father. Her name is connected only to her."

We passed the *dukhan* on the way out. "It makes you feel well and look well," said Fatima. "Your body gets strong." She showed us some acacia wood which she sometimes uses as sandalwood is so expensive, and then some of her perfumes. One of the bottles had a coarse, grainy sediment at the bottom of it. "It's made from crocodile scales," she said, and laughed at the look of horror on our faces.

She walked us to the gate, being careful to stand back from the view of any passer–by as she opened it. We said goodbye.

11 MOLLY

The sound of a high–pitched male voice half–singing, half–chanting filtered out from the house as I crossed the garden. Inside in all the rooms little bags were hanging from the walls. A trail of dried blood in the yard near the kitchen marked the spot where a sheep had recently been slaughtered.

Molly had recently moved house and all the usual traditions were being observed: the Koran being played all the time, little amulets in bags hung up to ward off the evil eye, gifts of entire sheep for the house–warming celebrations.

Molly had invited me round for coffee and a preliminary chat to see if she'd be willing to contribute to the book. At first glance she contrasted oddly with the Arab/Islamic sights and sounds in the background. No one could look more English.

Molly did not come to Sudan for reasons of religion. She was a Catholic when she arrived in the country with her Muslim husband and remained so for some time. But she took the road to Islam independently and is now more at ease there than in the UK.

I met Mubarak when he was studying in England and I was working part–time at a student hostel. I was studying but I was helping out there on Saturdays so I got to meet him and other Sudanese people there. I just got to know the Sudanese crowd quite well and I think it was after I'd known him for about a year we discussed that I might come to Sudan on holiday, when he came back here to live. So, I came back here and spent some time living in the family house. Just on holiday, just for a month. I think for him it was so that he could find out what I thought of

Sudan first and whether I could actually live here before making any decision to get married. And I think the father, who was a wise man, had sort of said, she should spend time here first before that decision is made.

So I spent about a month here and then I went back to England for a few months. Then I came back again and that's when we decided that we would get married. We had a traditional wedding here in Khartoum and then went back to England for an English sort of simple wedding ceremony for my parents. I thought it would be too much to bring them out here, with all the ceremony and all the three days of the wedding and the crowding in the houses.

If I remember, the first day was actually Mubarak's henna day when the man has the henna done and I remember just being with the ladies and they would decorate me with henna and such. That was a smaller day. He had his own party with the men and had henna on his hands. The second day was the traditional white wedding day where you wear your white dress and you sit on your thrones there and the people just come and say congratulations. I wouldn't say it was very enjoyable. It's not like in England where you have a nice dinner with family and whatever. You just end up with hundreds of people. You don't know who they are and you just really sit on a chair and people just keep on coming up and saying congratulations. There was a bit of dancing and you could have maybe a slow dance together. They expect you to do that with your husband towards the end.

I had my henna party on day three if I remember rightly, when they dressed me in gold and I had the henna done and I had a little go at the dancing and things. They decorated my legs and hands with henna but I didn't want too much, flowery patterns and things. And then I didn't have so much gold and I didn't want it bought for me so we actually borrowed gold from some relatives. So they covered me in gold but it wasn't mine and I only had a few pieces but it was a traditional thing and I was very keen just to try it out. I think, because it was different, it was fun. It was something exciting and different. You're just more or less dancing for the ladies that day but your husband does appear. He does come in some time in the evening and stands and watches you do the dance. I hadn't been taught to do the dance so I was just more or less having a go which I don't think I'd do now. I think the fact that I was just so young then, you know, you don't feel as shy. I would never do that sort of thing now.

We did something where we sat together on an *angaraib* taking mouthfuls of milk and then spitting it out over each other. I think people were just quite amused when that was being done because they thought I wouldn't know what was going on, so there was a lot of laughing and it was quite fun. I think Mubarak was saying no, no, no there's no need to do this or that but the women thought it was just hilarious because I didn't know what was going on and it was funny.

That day you wear more of a sleeveless dress. The idea is that because it's just for the ladies and your husband you're allowed to be a little bit more revealing – although my dress was quite long, it wasn't one of these short ones that they wear today, it was a bit longer but it was sleeveless and you were covered in gold.

They did the *halwa* for me, like a waxing, to have the hair removed, all the body hair. It's up to you really, you don't have to but you can. I think it's nice because in a hot country like this it's quite cool to have your body hair removed.

I was probably a bit confused about when I was actually married. I think it's actually the early evening of the white day where the men go to the mosque and the papers are signed. You're not involved in that in any way. So it does feel a bit strange. You're just sitting at home while the men go and sign the papers at the mosque. But then of course when we went to England we were married again. It was just a registry office wedding but papers are signed and then you get to sign so you actually feel you're married.

At that stage when I was first married I was still interested in all sorts of religions. So I still had my books on Hinduism and

Christianity. I used to read a lot because I was determined that I wasn't just going to get married and then convert. There was no way I would do that. I was a practising Catholic but I was very interested in other religions. I knew I probably would convert to be a Muslim and I wanted to read up on others because I wanted to be sure before. So I read up a lot about the different religions. And about a year after I married I converted.

Despite her surface appearance of quintessential Englishness, Molly feels more comfortable in Sudanese society, particularly as regards contact with men.

I've always been quite a shy person anyway, but I think as well, living in Sudan now so many years and being separated from men that I don't know…. I'm OK if it's a man that I know, like Mubarak's close friends. I'll sit and chat to them but I'm very shy around strangers. I think Sudanese women are not as shy actually. They're quite confident around men. But I'll just not feel happy sitting talking to men any more. It's just something that's come about in all the years.

Even now I don't like to walk down the street here in Sudan. I wouldn't do it. I would feel people were looking at me. I just wouldn't like to go for a walk here at all whereas I used to years ago. I think it's a bit of both, being a foreigner and being a woman. I don't like any attention being drawn to myself, and people here will stare, you being a foreigner and I just don't like the attention I guess. I don't consciously think, oh because I'm a Muslim I'm not going to walk down the street, it's just something I don't feel comfortable doing.

In the UK I'm just one of hundreds of people so I will do that no problem but if men came into the house I would shy away from them and probably if it wasn't necessary, if I didn't have to actually have a conversation with them, I'd go and sit somewhere else. Again I think it's a mixture of shyness and feeling that it's not right. With women I'm different, I guess. I've always been a shy person but I think it's increased more since I've become a Muslim.

I would like to wear the *hijab* and I think eventually I will but I think it's really just something that I've not been used to doing. I pray, and of course when I pray I wear the *hijab*. But then most of the time I'm not out very much, I'm around the house a lot. Maybe that's why I feel very shy when I'm walking out because I'm not wearing the *hijab*. I guess I know that I should and I hope one day that I will. I'm still very shy about it. I tend to always wear long. You'll find me always in a long skirt and normally I will wear long sleeves so really what I'm missing is just the headscarf. My job doesn't bring me into contact with men really because I work with little children. I don't go out that much unless it's maybe to school occasions to do with my own children.

I don't have a big social life really. I work in the mornings and then in the afternoons I'm helping my own kids with their homework and things. I do my visiting; relatives and things. I try to keep up with the Sudanese duties of going to family members. That's very important. And close neighbours. And if somebody's not well, or if there's a wedding or a funeral I do go to these things. But if we were to go out as a family, maybe once every couple of months we might go out for a meal, somewhere like the Hilton, the German club or something, but that's it really. There's not much entertainment.

Other than that, Mubarak, my husband, is very involved in commitments of going to all the funerals, all the people that are sick, all the weddings that I wouldn't go to, as I don't know as many people. I go to the very close relatives. He would be going to so many places that it would take almost every day to go out to these things if you do as you should and visit the people that are sick and such. It would be a daily thing. So every evening almost he's having to go out to something like that. Or some men will come to visit him, so he is mostly very occupied with these things.

We don't get to spend much time together. The time we spend together would be when we travel, when we go back to the UK, or sometimes we go to Dubai in December. Men can be very much lost in their commitments in Sudan, probably in a lot of Muslim countries.

With my children our family way is very Islamic and my daughter, for some reason, has been quite rebellious. It happens a lot with mixed marriages, the daughters tend to have a hard time for a while. I think it's against the rules and the strictness really. Maybe it's because she knows other things so for her she's not at all like I was as a teenager, she's a very strong and rebellious type. As I say, now she seems to be coming out of that but I think she had problems with identity more than anything. I think that has to do with a lot of issues. I think it has to do with colouring, because my husband's black and I'm white, so she's brown. She's in between, she doesn't fit totally with the Sudanese culture and she doesn't really fit totally in with the Western culture. So I think that's another issue altogether, prejudices maybe and culture differences.

Most of her friends are Sudanese, but they're mostly the modern type, the Western type, those that are on the way to being American girls, you know. But the boys are well–adjusted. I know with Samia she's calming down now, she seems to be getting a lot better. She was saying she wants to go abroad to study at 16, she wants to go to England, a lot of Sudanese girls do from the very modern, not so religious families. Her daddy has put his foot down, saying no, no, no, when you're older, maybe when you're 18 you'll go but not at 16. But the more he gets worried about things and panics and puts his foot down, the more she tries to fight and push to do what she wants.

I've been very lucky with my husband's family. I get on very well with them. His sisters are fairly modern really but religious at the same time. Mubarak is probably stricter than them but they've never sort of commented or said anything. I think, because I'm quite an old–fashioned person myself, my old–fashionedness almost matches their modernness, we meet somewhere on a road there.

I was very lucky in that my mother–in–law – she's dead now – was a very sweet lady. She was an educated lady. She was one of the first woman teachers in Khartoum and she was always so good to me really. She always sympathised with me. If ever I did have a slight – not quarrel, but – misunderstanding with any of Mubarak's sisters his mother would always side with me. I think they were a bit more understanding because they knew that I was a foreigner so they didn't ever gang up against me or anything. The mother and father would always be on my side really, and quite open–minded about things.

It had its advantages and disadvantages living in a family house. I think in a way I did enjoy the company of other people around. We were in a flat so it was good that we could go down and be with the family when we wanted and disappear from it when we wanted. Mubarak was the youngest son of the family and the older brother had left the house so he was required to be there with his mother and father and I don't think we would ever have moved to our own house had his mother and father still been alive. It's only the fact that they're dead that we've actually left the family house. When we did leave his sisters would come and sit and cry here almost every day. The fact that he'd left the family house even though he's married and has his own children. They thought it was just so sad that he'd left. Something disappears from the house once he's left.

I think I felt the lack of privacy at first. When I came to Sudan it was all a bit strange but I guess when you're coming from somewhere like England where you're living alone and things are very private…. It was nice for a while. There was a time when I loved it, living amongst the people. Then I think there was a time after I got married when I began to want my own space but there are a lot of advantages as well, living in a Sudanese house.

Funerals are a big thing in Sudan: they are prolonged, lasting at least three days; a large number have to be attended because of the extensive network of social contacts and the obligation that people have to put in an appearance even at the funerals of people they sometimes barely know.

The funerals are very shocking. When Mubarak's mother died a couple of years ago she died in the hospital. She'd had cancer. Somehow the hospital had managed to get all the family away from the hospital before they were told. I think they removed her from her room, they were taking her to intensive care and I think they told my husband that they should all go home for a little while and that they could come back in a little while. Because usually there's a bedside vigil of family when someone's ill here but somehow it was managed that they all got sent home. And then I was upstairs and suddenly I just heard a big uproar of screaming. You know it's quite terrifying when you hear it and then of course the house fills with hundreds of people in minutes. People just come and scream and scream together. What had happened was they'd contacted one of the relatives who would be able to tell the rest of the family, someone not so involved, not the son or daughter of the person who'd died. They'd told someone stronger and younger – it was a nephew actually – to come and tell them in the house because they know the commotion it causes here.

I don't know if this happens always because sometimes you do hear screaming going on in hospitals. But I think they generally prefer to get people out so it doesn't disturb the other patients and the other people that are there with their relatives. After about an hour or so of the screaming the body is brought in on an *angaraib*. It comes back into the house maybe just about an hour after dying and they go into a room where there are certain people, maybe a couple of close relatives, maybe a couple of daughters, and someone who knows about the washing of the body. This can be a relative or it can be a neighbour. Not everybody knows how to wash the body of the dead; there's only certain people that can. They wash it and there's certain oils they have to rub in and the body's wrapped in just a shroud and they block the nose and different parts with cotton wool. And that's all done and prayers said over the body. Anyone who's hysterical they don't let them in because there's a saying here – I don't know if it's Islamic – that the body continues to hear a little while after death so anyone who's hysterical is sent out of the room. And then the body's put back on the *angaraib*, wrapped up, and taken back through the screaming crowd and the men go and the ladies are left. They're not allowed to go, they're left screaming away and hysterical as the body's being taken away to be buried. And it's buried in the ground, facing towards Mecca, not in a coffin, just covered in a shroud. And it's not like in other religions where people would visit the grave. It's not really recommended that people go back to the grave very often. Sometimes they do just straight after the death but it's not somewhere that you go and say prayers or anything. Occasionally people might go but not often.

The *bika* goes on for three days afterward. The good thing about it is that people get to scream, get it all out of them, although in Islam it's not really recommended to do so. It's supposed to be that you shouldn't question God too much, so you always get the religious men coming to calm the ladies down and saying, you know, you shouldn't be doing this, you shouldn't be screaming. The men can genuinely cry loudly too, so they do get a lot of the grief out of their system. My husband did. It's something that Western men might not do as much. But as they're doing that they also have a hundred other things to think about. They've also got to feed and give drinks and tea to all these hundreds of people. And again, anything here in Sudan, weddings or funerals, you have to show good hospitality. You have to show what you have, you have to show that you are able to feed all these people. It would be a shame for them if they couldn't show that they were able to do that. So immediately also their mind is switched to organising. They get caterers in often, you still have to be alert enough to be able to greet people and know who you're greeting and ask after their family. So it's quite good in helping you get over a death because you've got to do certain things that are required of you.

Although in the first days and hours they are genuinely upset and screaming, you will find distant relatives coming in, or friends or neighbours, and they might join in, but they might not be as sincere as those people that are really, really crying. I think that the *bikas* here in Sudan are more a traditional thing really rather than religious. I think the Sudanese *bikas* are quite famous. You might find in the very strict religious families they're more controlled about these things.

The halal slaughter of animals often upsets non–Muslims. Even meat–eaters don't like seeing animals being killed and they believe it causes suffering. Muslims deny this. The knife used is sharper than a razor blade, they say, the slaughterers are very skilled, using a method prescribed in the Koran, and the animal loses consciousness immediately.

When I first came to Sudan I was quite shocked by seeing the sheep killed in that way. But then it was explained to me that they slit the throat in a certain way that they don't feel, that it'll be instantaneous, that it's just the nerves and things that carry on a few minutes after that. They come from behind and they say it's very quick and it's more humane. But nevertheless since I saw a sheep being killed I won't eat lamb here. It just makes me feel ill. In England I didn't see it so you don't really think you're eating meat whereas in Sudan I see the sheep, see it being killed, see the blood, so I don't want to eat it.

When we lived in the family house these things were easier because often there were occasions where they would slaughter sheep either to give thanks for something or somebody will give you a gift of a sheep and you're required to slaughter it. I think it's a very messy business. So living in a flat in a family house it was great because you didn't have to be involved in that. So when we moved here and we were being given gifts of sheep I accepted a few being done but last week another one was delivered and I just said, oh couldn't we please give it away, because it's just the mess and the smell and the flies and I'd rather give it to the poor than have to prepare it here, whereas my husband wanted to invite his family round and they'd all eat it.

You can take it along to the mosques and places like that. We've done it a lot where they slaughter it here and then the butcher cuts it up and divides it here and will give it out to the different mosques, then it will be distributed. They do the same with other types of food. I know that at certain times my husband will – I think it's called *belila*, the little bean things – they actually boil up a load of this and send that off to give it to the mosque, and also rice with milk, to be distributed to the poor, and there's a blessing in it.

There is nothing Molly finds particularly difficult about being a Muslim, not even the fasting that has to be done during Ramadan.

Do you know, I realise that it's part psychological really and that we drink and eat for different reasons. It's not just for being dry in the mouth, it's actually a comfort as well, to sit and have a cup of coffee or tea. I'm fasting today, I've been fasting the last five days because I'm making up days before the start of Ramadan. If you have your period you can't fast so I've got days owing. Because I have stomach ulcers I don't actually have to fast but because I've had these ulcers for so many years I've started the last few years fasting again. What I do is I get up before the morning prayer. Before the call at 5.20 am, you can eat and drink. So, by waking up at about 4.45 am, I eat something heavy, like a porridge or a Weetabix, or something that will lie heavy in your tummy, and then I just make sure I have my coffee and a good few glasses of water and some juice. My tummy will feel so full at that point. So during the day my mouth does feel dry but I actually psychologically know I've had something to eat and I've had lots to drink before 5.20 am. You can rinse your mouth and spit it out and you can brush your teeth and this makes a big difference so I feel absolutely fine. I went to exercise this morning and I was dreading that, thinking oh, fasting, exercising and sweating, how is that going to be, but I came in and immediately brushed my teeth and rinsed out my mouth and once you get rid of the dryness my insides feel absolutely fine. And then you try and make your day not too hectic in Ramadan and you give yourself a chance in the afternoon to take a nap and lie down in a cool room. But when you imagine when the Prophet Mohammed fasted in the desert, we're lucky to be living in cool houses. And I find having a cool bath helps. I find mornings are fine. I'll finish work and I'll jump in a cool bath, wash my hair, brush my teeth and then later on I'll go and have a lie down. So no, I don't find fasting difficult at all. It's psychological. You think it would be difficult but if you stock up just before the morning prayer you're stocked up and straight after breakfast in the evening you drink again. The only problem I think I maybe eat less in Ramadan. Some people can fast all day and like my husband sit down to breakfast without a sip. I will gulp down three big drinks of water which is wrong really because then you fill up like a balloon. And then you can't eat. So I'll maybe make up a milkshake of banana or something because I know it's fluid but there's some goodness in it as well. But I've not found it's done me any harm. I know my body's getting the same, probably even more, liquid than it would be when I'm not fasting, because when you're fasting you're conscious then during the evening to keep drinking, to keep some water beside you during the night, you wake up and you take a drink.

I try to make a special effort during Ramadan to get up for the first prayer because I would be up to drink and eat. Not everyone does. Some people can't get out of their beds. It's quite difficult actually. You're half asleep and you have to force yourself to eat and drink. Sometimes it's a bit of a struggle. But on those days during Ramadan I will be up for the first prayer before sunrise.

I must admit I'm a bit lazy. During the rest of the year I pray the first prayer as I rise, when the sun is up. But during Ramadan you try and make a special effort to be a bit better.

There are certain words, certain prayers that you recite each time. They're just ones that everybody prays each time, and then you can choose one of the *suras*, one of the chapters of the Koran that the Prophet has set. Now for someone like me whose Arabic is limited, I'm not so good and I haven't learned so many *suras* in Arabic. I read the Koran in English. I've learned the smaller *suras* in Arabic so someone like me will pick just the shortest of *suras* to say in my prayer. You're required to say one chapter, which is the opening chapter of the Koran, and then you choose another *sura*, any *sura* of any length, any chapter. So it's set prayers and then at the end of your prayer you can just sit and pray as a Christian would, and ask God, thank God; you can then say your own little askings or thankings.

I pray five times a day. I've always prayed since I turned to Islam. First of all you wash to get ready to pray, the *wudu*, which is more or less washing the hands and the face and the feet.

I've always prayed a lot. When I was a child we spent some years living with my grandmother in the family house in Ireland, so I think I've been prepared for Sudan. My mother and father were divorced so my sister and I went to stay with my grandparents. Things were very simple living on a farm, where you went to pump water from the well, toilet outside, so I think I was well prepared. And then my grandmother was very religious. In Ireland there was something called the angelus where the bells would ring – I think it was three times a day – and then you stopped what you were doing and you prayed. So I was into this routine, even as a young child. And my grandmother had this thing at night where we would all kneel down in a circle and we would all pray, and she would be up at six to go to church every day. I always think these old religious people, say the strict Catholics, are very similar to Islam. So I had this praying well within me even before I became a Muslim It was almost like a preparation for being a Muslim. I think it implanted something in me.

Some Muslims might say Islam is the only right religion and everyone else is going to hell, but it's how you interpret the Koran. There is a part in the Koran where it says that God will choose between the people of whatever religion. Especially here in Sudan you meet such good Christian people who have given up their lives to come and help here and I actually think that it is just sort of levels. I do think that Islam is one of the higher levels that you can go to in religion and I think you can even go up in Islam. I think you get the lower stages of Islam, which is probably where I am, but you can get people who take it on extremely, the whole life, very strictly.

I think it's very important to believe in God, very important, and the reason I believe that is because I always ask God to show me the way. There was a stage where I was going to church every day as a teenager. My grandmother died and after that I was so sad that I used to be in church almost every day praying for her. And all that time I also prayed for myself and for guidance because I always said to God: I don't want to get this wrong, it's so important to worship you in the right way and I want you to show me the right way. So that was my prayers for many years, you see.

None of Mubarak's friends forced Islam on me. What happened was I was quite a religious person and when Mubarak picked me up he would often have to get me from the church because I would have been praying for my grandmother or whatever. He had a very religious friend called Khalil who now is almost living in the mosque and people don't really see him any more. He's very much now one of the very, very strict Muslims. But me and him – he was also studying in England – we would sit and chat a lot about religion. So during that time of my prayers for God to guide me in the right way, there was me and Mubarak's friend, Khalil, chatting and chatting, arguing about religion all the time. I would tell him about my religion, he would tell me about his. It was really a healthy discussion and just through talking to him, I think, it just snapped that Islam was right for me. Although I didn't actually convert till after I got married, all the information was coming into me before I got married. And it wasn't from Mubarak, it was from his friend who was a very religious person. We kind of hit it off because we both had religion very much on our minds.

He came back to Sudan and he did visit us quite a bit at first, and we used to talk about religion. That was before I became a Muslim. After I became a Muslim he didn't come as he then came to another level of religion. He's very strict now. He's really involved with the mosque and teaching the poor, one of these very true people. He gives up everything for the poor and for spreading Islam. And he dresses as the Prophet did with the short *jellabiya* and the sandals and the long beard.

It's not that he's avoiding us. I saw him once at an occasion Mubarak had but he wouldn't now be into parties, weddings, even funerals. The very religious people don't go to the funerals as much. They might pass by and just say sorry and pass on. They try to stay away from the traditional Sudanese customs. They devote themselves. I would class it as very similar to a nun or a priest really. They're trying to live as the Prophet lived, they're trying to be as the Prophet was. If you read any works on the Prophet, you'd be surprised. He was a very simple person who would sit and sew his own clothes and always open his door to the poor, always give to the poor. But I think just the fact that I'd prayed so hard to be guided, that's my proof, and that's why I became a Muslim, because I don't believe that God would guide me wrongly.

12 MOHAMMED ABDUL QAADIR

Mohammed Abdul Qaadir, previously Darrell Strong, is the son of black American middle–class parents, both of them academics. Although his parents divorced when he was still very young, the family members have always maintained close and supportive relationships.

He is a smallish man with a round face and there is something very boyish about him. He has a frank, cheerful and eager to please manner which is eclipsed by an air of fervid certainty whenever religious matters are discussed.

Generally I had a very good childhood. Most of it was spent in California, in Oakland, California in particular. I guess living in Oakland influences one. It's a very historical site. I guess you could say it's the home of revolutionary thought in the black community. That's where the Black Panthers started. We encountered racism sometimes and things like that but we dealt with it. Then when I was about 15 we moved to Detroit, Michigan.

Detroit, Michigan is a very interesting city. It's predominantly black. You see a lot of black upper middle–class people, educated African–Americans. It also has the largest Arab population outside the Middle East. There I had my first exposure to an Islamic community although I was very much an outsider. I saw Muslims and it interested me. As I got older I read the autobiography of Malcolm X. This book was very inspiring, eye–opening, because the things he was talking about in the book you could see right there. There's a lot of poverty in Detroit.

Also in Detroit I saw the Nation of Islam and this is where I began to become politically conscious and aware of the issues of the world and the black community. I was very pro African–American and very concerned about issues of African–American rights and equality and things like that. So finding the Nation of Islam was interesting. They appealed to me because they had discipline. Generally you would see them very organised, very clean–cut, very well groomed and unwilling to tolerate any inequality or any injustice. And they seemed to be very active in the black community. I'd heard about them in Detroit, I'd heard about them in other cities where they'd kind of cleaned up the communities. The Nation of Islam was interesting outwardly but inwardly I was aware that their ideas were completely ignorant and lacked spiritual substance. So I just saw them as a political movement like any other group that's around.

As a child Mohammed accompanied his mother to church. In her spiritual quest she tried several churches, all with African–American congregations.

My mother seeking spiritual enlightenment made me realise this was important. She and her friends were very spiritually inclined. She liked the excitement of the church but eventually she outgrew it. My father wasn't interested in religion. I never discussed it with him. The traditional black church is full of African women but no men generally. This is one of the biggest failures of the black church: it has failed to bring in men.

The main influence on me was my mother. She taught me that Jesus was a Prophet of God, not the son of God. We also went to the Catholic church with my stepmother but I got nothing from it. I would not participate. I had made the self–statement that to participate would be to affirm the trinity. Although I had not become a Muslim at this point I had clearly gravitated towards the beliefs of Islam. After reading Malcolm X, I was feeling like, OK I'm Muslim, and I told myself I'm going to become Muslim. I didn't become Muslim in Detroit. Why? Because I didn't know how to get in touch with the community.

At this time I was about 17 or 18. I would see Muslims outside what I know now to be the *masjid*. They were African–American, I know now, but at the time I saw them as Africans, maybe. They weren't Arabs and they clearly weren't Nation of Islam; they were wearing *jellabiyas* or Pakistani clothing and they had big beards. I hadn't seen African–Americans like this so I was thinking to myself, wow, I couldn't be with the Nation of Islam, and this group here, it's very interesting but I couldn't see myself fitting in with them because they were wearing *jellabiyas*. So I was kind of stuck, wondering – how do I get into Islam?

Other religions were not for me. It had to be Islam because it had the discipline I needed. I said to myself, I need discipline in my life but I need a system. The only thing that is complete is Islam. My mother says that she influenced me. She had a student who became Muslim, Derek, or Abdul Malik as he was now called. He was a very active student, very revolutionary on the campus. He became the leader of the *masjid* later. He was a good person with a lot of qualities. My mother said if you become like him, not necessarily Muslim, but with his qualities, I would be very proud of you.

At that point I graduated from high school. The school I wanted to go to was in Louisana, a Jesuit Catholic school, predominantly black and famous for the number of black students they sent to medical school. Many African–Americans were searching for some kind of black experience at that time; they didn't feel black enough so they wanted to go to one of these black schools. I didn't feel like that. I was very confident and secure with my roots. I went there to major in biology and go to medical school. I was interested in psychology and wanted to be a psychiatrist.

My growth in Islam stopped there. I didn't see a Muslim in the streets, didn't see a *masjid*. I got misdirected in a sense through university activities – women and things like that. I would go to parties but I never smoked and I drank just daiquiris with a little bit of alcohol. But I felt New Orleans to be very spiritually dead.

My mother visited me at the time of Mardi Gras. She said it was spiritually dead, that the vibes she got were not good vibes. She wanted me to leave.

At the same time my father moved to California State University. So I could go there for free. It was very tempting and I did that in the summer of 1996. Then my Islam started again, the very same summer I arrived in California. I immediately went to Abdul Malik's community, his *masjid*, and basically sat with him and I told him I had been reading about Islam and stuff like that and told him I was interested in becoming Muslim. He gave me a red book and told me to come back after I had read it. Maybe I was a little disappointed because I was ready to be a Muslim that very day. I went back the following Friday to the *masjid*, it was the time of the Friday prayer. There were a lot of people. I arrived a little late, just when they had finished the sermon. After the people had left I went to the *imam*, Abdul Malik, and told him I had read the book and I was ready to make the *shahada*. Abdul Malik said the *shahada* in Arabic and in English. I repeated this after him. At the very moment I really felt that I was a Muslim. I felt that I had entered into a worldwide community of one billion people, very diverse, various people from Arab countries, Asian countries, Europeans, Mexicans, Americans.

My mother knew all along I was going to accept Islam. We often had discussions about it. She was very interested and very encouraging of my intention. My brother Mark, he encouraged me also. My father, I didn't see him as often as I would have liked to, but on various occasions we would discuss Islam and he was supportive. My grandmother was also very supportive. Nobody was hindering me or discouraging or had any negative feelings towards my accepting Islam.

The climate of feeling about Islam in the States then was not like it is now. It was a considerable amount of time before the issues of Muslims and terrorism came into the media. At that time Palestinians and Israelis were at a very heated period, a volatile point, and there was a lot about Afghanistan, shortly after the

Taliban had come into control, but not to say that it would affect anybody's views about Islam, at least in my family.

The community I entered was considered very radical. They labelled themselves as revolutionary, and the community and the leader of the community tried to pattern themselves after the Black Panthers. Abdul Malik grew up in the setting of the Panthers. He was very influenced by them politically and by Malcolm X. He thought we should take Islam to the black community and use it as a vehicle to uplift the black community and strengthen the family in the black community. I agreed with him. I fit right in to the programme at this *masjid*.

There were other Muslim communities in Oakland, some that were attended by immigrant Muslims, from Arab countries, Palestine, Yemen or Somalia maybe. I visited them and met many people there but my main community was the African–American community of *Masjid* Islam. It was very distinct from the others in that it was not pro–assimilationist. They wanted to establish Islam in America whether it be through the establishment of an Islamic community that is independent of America and its laws or whether it be by just an overwhelming majority of American people accepting Islam and thereby the government changes itself. It was different in that the other African–American community was very assimilationist. They wanted to assimilate with the government and they were generally very ignorant of the atrocities the American government had committed and continued to commit against the African–American people. Perhaps they were aware of them but they kind of followed a Martin Luther King philosophy and the *Masjid* Islam followed a Malcolm X philosophy.

I wouldn't say that my lifestyle changed a lot. My opinions about political issues didn't change, but Islam helped me to articulate them better and to have a greater understanding of world issues, not just political issues. Islam helped me to deepen my insight.

I felt myself outgrowing the community I was in. I wanted to learn Arabic, I wanted to learn how to read the Koran and gain a deeper understanding of Islam beyond the general etiquettes of Islam. Some of us felt we had reached a level that we weren't increasing any more. We wanted knowledge and we felt that this community wasn't offering it to us. At that time there were two Muslim teachers, one African–American, one European–American. Hamza Yusuf, the European–American, had travelled to Mauritania and Morocco, Mohammed Sherif, the African–American, to Sudan. They had begun to offer classes on Islamic jurisprudence, or *fiqh*, which covers the everyday dealing of Muslims, whether it be prayer, fasting, Haj, giving alms, business transactions, marriage, all of these aspects of Islamic life were covered. I began to attend their classes. They were teaching us jurisprudence and *tasawwuf* (purification of the heart, spiritual purification). *Tasawwuf* is a science like other sciences of Islam and generally people call it Sufism. It's the science of purifying the heart from blameworthy characteristics. This was the first time we had gained deep spiritual insight into Islam and its ways rather than the external actions.

It was at this point that Mohammed discovered the teachings of Sheikh Uthman Dan Fodio, a Sufi scholar and preacher of the Qadiriyya tariqa, who was instrumental in reviving the spirit of Islam in Nigeria in the 18th and early 19th centuries. When conflict rose between Dan Fodio and the secular ruler he and his followers withdrew to an area outside government control and set up an Islamic state, the Sokoto Caliphate, from where they conducted a jihad against unbelievers. Dan Fodio was a prolific writer, producing well over 100 books on Islamic science that are still widely read today. One of his most well–known books is Bayan wujub al hijra, hijra being the journey a Muslim makes from a land which is not conducive to the practice of Islam to one which is. The word was first used in Islam to refer to the migration of Prophet Mohammed, away from the persecution he was experiencing in Mecca, to Medina where he could establish an Islamic state.

MOHAMMED ABDUL QAADIR

Mohammed Sherif was teaching these books written by Sheikh Uthman. Then he started on *Bayan wujub al hijra*, so he was teaching a book about all the obligations of *hijra*.

Uthman Dan Fodio wrote this book to encourage his followers to make *hijra*. In America and all over the world we are living in an oppressive state in that we are not governed by Islam, we are governed by non–Muslim laws and non–Muslim leaders and it's oppressing us in that we are not able to practise Islam and the *sharia* of Islam in its totality. This book explained when it is obligated for a person to make *hijra*, when it is recommended and when it is a neutral position.

Mohammed Sherif was basically suggesting that Muslims in non–Muslim lands should make one of two choices: either they should establish a Muslim community within the non–Muslim land or they should emigrate to a Muslim land.

We learned it is not permissible for a Muslim to live in a land of disbelief, where the government is not Islamic, where there is sexual corruption and all other forms of corruption, where you are not able to manifest Islam. If we wanted to grow spiritually, and attain the highest levels of Islam we had to leave America.

Mohammed Sherif was a follower of a Sufi sheikh, Sultan el Haj Abu Bakr Mohammed Tahir in Sudan. The Sultan, as Mohammed calls him, is a descendant of Uthman Dan Fodio. He lives in the village of Maierno in Sennar.

We wanted to go deeper into the spiritual purification and we wanted to join a brotherhood that would give us a methodology for doing so. Mohammed Sherif said it is better to go to Sudan and take the *tariqa* from the Sultan. I myself came to a point where I said I am going to make *hijra* and study Islam. I had stopped school and was working to make money to travel. I had come to a point where everything I was learning in university was contrary to what I was learning in Islam. I had met a Muslim psychologist from Spain. His method was somewhat Islamically oriented. I decided I wanted to gain a Koranic perspective of psychology and I realised I had to leave America to study. I was looking for a spiritual teacher I could sit with one–on–one. I wanted to live and establish a family and Sudan was what fit.

My departure was very sudden. I had a friend who also wanted to leave and he came to me and said we could get a good deal on a ticket to Egypt through a stewardess, a one–way ticket to Cairo for $200. But we had to leave within a week. I sold my car for $2,000 and I had a couple of cheques from work coming. And basically I left. I went to see my father, it was such an abrupt decision it was really hard. We went to a restaurant, we had lunch and here I am, telling him I'm going to be leaving in about four days. He started crying and I started crying too. It was a very emotional time. I think about it a lot. But it was something I really had to do. The problem was I couldn't give him a satisfactory explanation of why I had to do it. He was concerned that I was going to get involved with, or was maybe already involved with, some kind of terrorist organisation or something like that. So I tried to ease his feelings about that, that no, I wasn't involved with anything like that, nor did I have the intention to do so. It was definitely not my goal. I just kept trying to help him realise it was something that I had to do for myself spiritually. I would come back at some point maybe. I left it open. The conversation ended up more as a conversation about politics. He studied international relations, he's a professor in political science. He knows a lot about the Muslim world and stuff like that, he knows about Islamic principles and stuff. But I was unable to really get him to understand why I had to leave. My mother on the other hand was very happy but very sad that I had to leave. She understood more why I wanted to leave but she kind of had in her mind that I would go for a year and then come back. That's the way she wanted to see it. My brother, I talked to him on the phone. Nobody was telling me I couldn't go but nobody was understanding 100 per cent.

My friend and I left one morning and we arrived in Egypt. November 98, I think. When we got to the airport in Cairo there was no sign of the Sudanese guy who was supposed to meet us. I spoke absolutely no Arabic. My friend spoke a little so he did our communicating, to the taxi driver. We ended up staying the first night in a hotel in the Azhar area near the Islamic University. Eventually we managed to contact the Sudanese guy and we went to his house to stay. We were staying with a lot of young Sudanese boys who were fleeing the country because they didn't want to serve in the army. They were studying in Egypt or waiting to get visas for America or Canada or somewhere. So we always had this debate, they wanted to flee and we wanted to go where they were coming from. They told us a lot of bad things about Sudan, that the people were very poor, that they had no food. But it just reaffirmed the fact that we wanted to go. They were good people, they were nice but they were young and they didn't know much about their religion and we wanted to go to Sudan even more so.

Although it had always been their intention to go to Sudan, getting a visa was proving to be difficult. After a couple of months, and with their money running out, they began to consider other options.

Egypt was a difficult place. We encountered a lot of racism, especially my friend, who's darker than me. In general there was a lot of what we call in Arabic *fasaad* in Egypt, a lot of corruption and a lot of promiscuity in the streets, a lot of women who were openly prostituting. We tried to see if we could start teaching English but that was difficult. We found a couple of English institutes but they had pretty strict requirements so that wasn't a possibility. We thought about advertising but we were a little hesitant to do so because of the nature of the government there. We didn't want to draw attention to ourselves because they might think that we were teaching Islam or trying to do something political. We had an Egyptian friend who told us we were being followed by the Egyptian secret police and it soon became obvious to us that we were. Our Egyptian friend stopped hanging around us. Even if we saw him in the street he would just keep walking. To Egyptians we seemed to be very Islamic religious people and the government, they kind of follow anybody that comes that way. We thought about Saudi but we couldn't get a visa. We wanted to stay in Africa because we knew that we could study the Maliki school of thought in Africa. So we considered going to Nigeria and Chad but we didn't have enough money for the plane tickets. We wanted to stay in an Arab country also because we wanted to learn the language. So we thought about Morocco but again it was too expensive. Jordan was nice but expensive. So it was clear that Syria was the only option.

Between the two of us we had just enough money to get to Syria. We didn't need any money there because we were enrolled in a programme that was basically free and they provided you with a room and board. It was a complete Islamic school sponsored by a Syrian sheikh, what you call a *mufti*, an Islamic judge for the Syrian government, sponsored through his benevolence. His name was Sheikh Ahmed Kuftara. There were other Americans coming as well because Syria was like a middle point. For those who didn't want to make *hijra* it was a good place because of its modernity. It wasn't exactly America but nor was it like Sudan where there was absolutely no infrastructure. So many of the Westerners came to Syria, and Syria had many options for studying. This was very attractive and was the main reason why we went there. Syria was a very affordable place. I stayed two years. I started teaching English and earned some money. But African–Americans encounter a lot of racism there. And the government was very un–Islamic. It all strengthened our determination to get to Sudan.

With the help of a Sudanese friend Mohammed finally obtained a tourist visa for Sudan. On his arrival he stayed with the friend's family in Omdurman, a vast village–like conurbation which sprawls over the left bank of the Nile, across from Khartoum.

It was a typical Sudanese family, from the Shaigia tribe, father, mother, three sisters, brother, grandmother, uncle – that was basically the family unit in the house. From them I learned a lot about Sudan, I picked up the local dialect, Sudanese eating customs, food and whatnot. I really liked Sudan right from the moment I landed. I felt that I was at home. I felt like I had finally made it, that I was free, that I was in control of myself. I felt very good spiritually, and it was Ramadan and I was able to intensify in my worship of Allah.

After two weeks I went to Sennar with an American friend. The whole time since I'd arrived I was just waiting, waiting to go to Sennar. We caught a bus which took about four hours to get there. We got off at Maierno, the village where my sheikh is, the Sultan, and we went to the Sultan's guest house. Basically it's an open courtyard, nothing fancy, nothing very lavish. You have no idea that you're at a sultan's house, it's just an ordinary place. Most of the people just have mud houses, there are no paved roads.

At this point, when I got off the bus, it was the first time I really felt I was in Africa. When I landed in this village I could sense the spirituality of the village, we say in Arabic, the *baraka*, I guess you could say the blessedness. It felt alive spiritually. That's what I'm trying to say, and the closer we got to the Sultan's guest house this feeling just increased. It was a very laid back place, you didn't see a lot of people, you didn't see a lot of women. Very laid–back.

When I finally met the Sultan I shook his hand and I said: *As salaam aleikum, ya sultan*. I was very pleased and overjoyed. He was just as my friends had described him. He was a tall man, a very humble man. You'd feel very comfortable with him. He's a very polite person, very sociable. But at that particular time he wasn't speaking. As a sultan, generally the greater part of the day he does not speak at all, from the morning until the evening prayer he does not speak. This is a spiritual exercise of his in that he remains silent in order to concentrate on his remembrances of Allah. He would give gestures and smile and you could see that he was very happy and elated to meet with me. He would oftentimes use gestures to ask questions or communicate with those around him. Everybody understands and this has been his routine for a very long time.

We got settled in the guest house, it was very comfortable. Sudan is a very simple place so we didn't have air–conditioning and things like that and the bathroom of course was outside but all of that I didn't have a problem with. Many people said that Sudan would be very hard but I think my ability to deal with Sudan was made much easier for me because I'd been in Syria and Egypt. There really wasn't anything I couldn't deal with.

I spent a lot of time with another sheikh called Farouk, who's like the spiritual representative of the Sultan. He had a lot of advice to give us about our spiritual affairs, what to do and what not to do. And the Sultan, whenever I found him not busy or not isolating himself I would spend time with him as well.

Farouk was the one that we accepted our *wird* from, the litany where we say *la illaha illa alla* a certain amount of times and we make a prayer on the Prophet a certain amount of times. He explained that one should say it in an audible voice but a very low voice. It should be done after every prayer and one should really try to concentrate on what one is saying with one's tongue so that one feels it inwardly and although it's on one's tongue one wants to say it to the point where these words really take root in the heart and one can begin to be affected by the meaning and by the benefit of this. He would also give us general advice on prayers, having humility before Allah in our prayer and in our daily contact with people, to avoid arguing with people. He would give us advice through his general comments on what might be taking place around us. We would learn through his character and the way he dealt with other people. Here in Islam the etiquette that one has with one's sheikh is that one listens and doesn't speak and doesn't ask a lot of questions other than questions that are absolutely necessary, and one just benefits from the teacher's behaviour rather than trying to ask a lot questions and get a lot of information. Generally the sheikh, if he's able to relate to you, will give you what you need as you need it and not more than that, like if I asked him how much Koran should I read every day he would tell me to do something very simple, knowing that if I were to take on something more or something difficult I would not be able to continue it for a long period of time.

Mohammed spent a few weeks in Maierno before travelling on to another village, Mabruka, which has a famous programme of Islamic studies.

The Sultan is basically my spiritual teacher and he teaches by way of example. He doesn't give lessons in *fiqh* and other things so he's not a teaching sheikh in that sense. In Mabruka there's a famous *khalwa* and they have a very thorough and comprehensive programme for studying Islam

Eventually after Ramadan I went for a visit. This other village has its own *tariqa*, its own spiritual brotherhood - the Tigani brotherhood. I didn't have any interest in leaving what I was already with as I was very happy with my spiritual path and happy with my sheikh. So I asked him to simply write a letter of introduction for me so he could explain that I had the *tariqa* with him and to clarify that I wasn't interested in taking another *tariqa* or anything like that, that I was only there to study and that there wouldn't be any kind of doubt what my intentions were.

It was a difficult ride to Mabruka because you can't reach it by the regular buses, you have to take one of those big metal trucks that people ride on the back. The village is very isolated. They don't have electricity and they pump water from a well on the outside of the village. They have a very, very small market, you can only get the basic things you need. All the women wear the *niqab* and you don't see them walking in the streets. Most of the people are from Western Sudan and they migrated there as part of a spiritual goal to establish Islam and to educate themselves in Islam. Basically they had all gone through a kind of *hijra*, although a *hijra* from one part of Sudan to another.

It's a very strict village. Everybody's expected to pray and to study in the study circles they have. That's what sets this village apart and that's why I chose it, because it's centred around studying Islam. And they have a very good programme for women. On every street there is a *zawiya*, a meeting house, where the women of that street go to study the Koran and to study Islamic books for *fiqh* and *hadith*, and so the women are very educated.

There is no better place for a Muslim to be than a village like this. All of your time is spent basically in worship of Allah. There is nothing to distract you. You get up early in the morning and right after the morning prayer you study, you then take a break and then go to your house. For those who have families, they have to meet the needs of their families by working. They do farming, some people work in the *souk*, other people travel outside the village for other work. They lead regular lives like other Sudanese people. They've just made certain choices to protect themselves and their families and to increase themselves in their worship of Allah.

I benefited greatly there. I stayed for three months, just studying the books of Islamic law and *hadith* and attending the circles of *fiqh*. Being there – although I liked studying there – reaffirmed my decision to be with the sheikh that I had chosen, in that I found him to be more exemplifying of the spiritually enlightened people of the past, more exemplifying of the practices of the spiritual elite. I was convinced that definitely my spiritual education would come from Maierno, but my education in terms of Islamic law I would take from Mabruka. Mabruka was also a place I wanted to go because these people are known for inviting non–Muslims to Islam. They often made trips to the south, to Southern Sudan, to central Africa or other surrounding countries to convert people to Islam and they've been very successful at doing it. So I wanted to go there as at that point it was somewhat my intention to return to America to give *da'awah*. Ever since I had left America it was my

intention to basically learn Islam, learn Arabic and to return back
to America, not to live, as I had basically chosen to live in Sudan,
but I wanted to return to America to share with the Muslims
in America what I had learned and also to invite non–Muslims
to join Islam, for example, non–Muslims on university campuses
and in other areas and particularly African–Americans. I think a
person is easily heard by his own people, or is most effective in
giving *da'awah* when he is giving *da'awah* to his own people.

I wanted also to return to Maierno with these studies and to try
to revive these traditional teachings there and make it a place like
Mabruka. Because Maierno has somewhat declined spiritually,
the youth are very distracted and are not grounded in Islam.

I left Mabruka because some brothers from America and Sweden
had come to Sudan and I had left to greet them. I would have
to be the communicator between them with the Sultan and with
others. I found them to be very happy to be in Maierno, in Sudan.
We discussed the future of our *jama'at* in Sudan and in America,
all of them had the intention to make *hijra* to Sudan in the future.
After one month I returned to Mabruka for two months. They
were having a leadership conflict, and it was annoying to me in
that it really hindered the studies because it was a big dispute and
the village had divided.

Had I been by myself I'd have stayed but at this point one of
the people who had come to Sudan had left a young boy of about
13 in my care and he went to Mabruka with me in order to study
the Koran there. Although he would of course have preferred to
be in America with his family Amir realised that his father had
sent him here to accomplish a goal, and he was very set on doing
that, he was eager to do that, and I didn't want this to be affected
by the problems in the village just because all the studies had
stopped for a period of time. So we both left and went back to
Maierno. We wanted to leave him in Maierno because that was
the best place for him. He was with people who loved him, he
was learning Arabic. His father converted over twenty years ago
so he was born into a Muslim family. Although I wanted to leave

him in Maierno, there wasn't a properly organised *khalwa* there. I wanted to find a *khalwa* for the boy where he would basically twenty–four hours a day be on the premises of the *khalwa* and memorising the Koran. So we came to Khartoum and I continued my studies with a personal teacher in Omdurman and put the boy in a *khalwa* there. So the boy was living in the *khalwa* and I went again to live with the Sudanese family who I had been living with. Amir would come to me on the weekend and we would go to visit Askari. Sometimes we would go and eat pizza or if there was an opportunity to watch a decent movie, not at the cinema but if I could rent a video, we'd maybe watch a movie or something like that. He was benefiting greatly. And this boy, Amir, his coming to Sudan and staying here was like an experiment. Because if he was able to survive and do well other families in America would send their children and myself and Askari would look after them. We intended to make a *khalwa*, a very formal and organised and disciplined *khalwa* in Maierno.

This is our foremost goal, it addresses our educational needs not only for the adults who will come here but also for the children. We want to design a *khalwa* in order to have a more Islamic–centred education, in which Koran and the memorisation of it is the first thing that a child learns. This is in line with traditional Islamic education in that when he reaches 7 years old the child begins to memorise Koran. We feel this is the first step to the revitalisation of Islam, as individuals, as an Islamic community and for the Islamic nation internationally. Memorisation of the Koran in the primary years, until maybe 10, 11, 12. The child will then study Islamic law, the books of *fiqh*. This would educate the child in everything that he is obligated by Allah to know, everything that he needs to know to function in society, in order to do what is permissible and avoid that which is not permissible. In traditional Islamic education this includes mathematics, geography etc., the usual school subjects.

Our long term goal is to establish a school, our short–term one is to establish a *khalwa* – for my children, for the local children of Maierno and for the children of other Americans who we hope will come to Sudan.

The first step will be to acquire land in Maierno. We made a proposal with costs and plans, and the goal is that it would become self–supporting through farming or through other financial ventures. The boys would live on the site and would go home on the weekend. We want to maintain a certain level of discipline and to ensure that the kids will be able to reach the goal that they are expected to meet, to memorise Koran. Many *khalwa*s have become places for children whose parents can't control them. Or for boys who want to avoid national military service. Eventually we can expand into a school or an institute where we can teach other subjects. Koran first, then jurisprudence, then other subjects and then the boy will be prepared for his life, he will be prepared to answer Allah on the day of judgement. We want the medium to be English and Arabic; Arabic as it is the language of Islam and English because students will then be able to become inviters to Islam through the medium of English because it is an international language.

Mohammed's wife gave birth to their first child during the period of our interviews. His wife is the niece of his sheikh, the Sultan. He had married her about eighteen months previously, shortly after her 16th birthday.

In terms of marriage it's a very common topic of discussion among the foreigners here in Sudan whether or not it's better to marry a woman who is, say, educated in the university or a woman who has little education. Generally the reason is that being from America we desire a woman who we can relate to and with whom we can talk about international issues, politics, Islam at a very high level, that sort of thing. One would think that one could do this with a woman who has received a university education. However, I guess we have found that this is not necessarily the case, whether it's because they don't have the aptitude or just that they simply haven't thought about many of these things. And generally speaking we have observed that those that have been college educated here in Sudan are going to aspire towards career ambitions. So a woman who has been college educated, we'd generally be going in opposite directions because we've left America, we're trying to live in Sudan, we're even trying to leave Khartoum and live a very simple life in Maierno or in whatever village it might be. And we find that women who have been educated in university aren't necessarily willing to do that. Most of the women become secretaries or accountants or something like that and if I was going to allow my wife to work outside the home I wouldn't allow her to work in such a job, around other men. I don't have a problem with her working but it has to be a job that is suitable and where Islamic principles can be observed and maintained in the work environment. On the other hand, a woman who hasn't been educated, perhaps she can't discuss with us international issues, she has no awareness of what happens in America, or, the latest about what's going on in Palestine maybe, but we see that as more positive than negative. She doesn't know it and she doesn't really have a desire to know it. Her concerns are basically her immediate life, her family, her husband, her parents, and this is actually more in line with what we want.

I married a woman from Maierno because I just found it easier to marry from people I have a relationship with and I have a relationship with the people of Maierno. In Islam you don't just simply start making contact with a woman and go through a dating process and things like that, you generally go through a member of her family or someone who searches for a wife for you. When I arrived in Sudan I knew that I wanted to get married and I got married about a year later. The first woman I was going to marry actually was about a year older than me and she was college educated. She studied Islam and she was very knowledgeable and very religious. As far as that was concerned she was the ideal woman for me. However there were simple differences that we couldn't come to agreement on. Those were issues of education for children, where we would live, things like that. Although those things weren't necessarily things that would keep me from marrying her they were obstacles. From the beginning of my conversations with her there was a little bit of doubt.

She worked in a telephone centre. I saw her and I asked my sheikh's brother about her because the telephone centre is owned by my sheikh's brother. And he simply said, OK I know her and I will talk to her father, and after that meeting with her father I met her. I wasn't aware of her age at the beginning but I found this older sister to be very set in her ways, very set on following Sudanese tradition in many aspects of life and for that reason I decided I wouldn't marry her.

Then I asked one of my sheikh's other brothers, who I had made a close relationship with, if I could marry his daughter. I had never seen his daughter but I knew him to be a good man, a man of piety, so I figured his family must be a pretty well–mannered family, his daughters should be well–mannered, they should understand the etiquettes of the woman in marriage and they should be religious. I was aware that he had two daughters that were ready to get married. One had just gotten engaged and the other was ready to get married. He told me she was 15, and I thought that was good; although she was young, actually it was preferable to me. He basically informed her that somebody had asked for her in marriage, so later he set up a meeting. Originally when I talked to her she said she was too young to get married. She told me, I'm only 15. She was very shy, she didn't look me in the eye at that first meeting. Slowly as we met a little more she was able to talk to me more. She didn't object to getting married and I found her to be suitable. We laugh about it now but I had actually seen her one time before. She was sweeping up the yard of the museum they were setting up for the artefacts associated with *hijra*, their swords and their spears, all of the original books and documents that some of the *muhajiroun* came with from Nigeria. Later I found out that she used to cook for me. I would stay in the guest house of my sheikh, and the woman who is now my wife used to prepare the food.

I was 27, turning 28, at the time. My sheikh's daughter got married the same day that I did so we made a double wedding. It was simple. I didn't make a lavish marriage like many Sudanese do. My father–in–law and his brother slaughtered two cows and we had a very nice lunch with a lot of people and family members from various areas. And because these people follow the *sunna* of Prophet Mohammed, I knew that not only was I going to find a good wife but everything was going to go in accordance with Islam: they weren't interested in taking money from me or selling their daughter, they weren't interested in parties or anything like this. So I married very happily.

At that point I didn't have a house there of my own, I simply stayed in the house of a friend for a week to have kind of like a honeymoon I guess you could say. Then I returned back to Khartoum to work and she just went back to her parents' house. I had already bought land in Maierno and my intention was to build a house and she would live there and I would go back and forth. However I found it difficult to go back and forth actually so eventually I found a house to rent in Khartoum and I went back and I got my wife and two of her aunts came with us. Normally in Sudan you have a family member of the woman, an aunt or maybe a sister, to help you in the house, to do cooking for you, cleaning, things like that. Me and my wife from the beginning we had a pretty good relationship. We opened up a dialogue. There were no hindrances in communication as people might expect when they think of people from two different nationalities getting married. I spoke Arabic. I could understand her and she could understand me. We did have things to talk about. I found her personality to be very much like my personality, no conflict, no pet peeves or anything like that.

Marriage to a person one has not had a chance to get to know or who has been chosen by other family members is a feature

*of other cultures which Westerners find difficult to understand.
Mohammed had no problem with this.*

When you consider that in the west 50 per cent or more of
marriages end in divorce it's clear that that way, getting to know
the girl before marriage, isn't necessarily the best way. I love her
in that she follows Islam and she is very Islamic, and of course
there is the general love that grows between two people. But,
you know, it takes time and I've noticed various stages in our
relationship as it has grown. Initially when we got married we
had a relationship where we could communicate and then after
she came to Khartoum with me the relationship grew of course.
We had a period when she was ill and we were going to the
hospital and she could see that I cared about her greatly. Then
of course she became pregnant, which increased the intensity of
the relationship.

I have a very good relationship with her father and a very good
relationship with her mother. Basically I have found a second
family. We're like one big family. They accept me, they really like
me and I really like them and I don't have any problems.

Because she was young, she hadn't reached the point where
she had found her own personality and wanted to do the things
that many other girls were doing which is somewhat negative,
actually, making themselves appear attractive for men, going to
parties. She hadn't quite reached that stage. So I was fortunate
that I had found her before that had taken place and that she
would be willing to accept the Islamic lifestyle that I wanted to
build together with her. You know, it wouldn't be a matter of
tearing down negative things and trying to make progress along
an Islamic path.

For a Muslim, the relationship between a man and a woman
is clearly defined, the relationship between a man and his wife
is clearly defined, the relationship between a man and a woman
who is not his wife is clearly defined, so all of this is clearly
defined and I see it as the most suitable way for humankind to

be productive and not be distracted by lowly desires. So although Sudan is a good place, I find Sudanese men don't care much for protecting their women and preventing them coming into contact with other men and that should be something that all Muslim men do. It's a level of jealousy that is positive, that every man should have for his mother, his wife, his sister, every woman of his family. At the same time he shouldn't allow himself to enter into unnecessary contact with women, flirting and you know. If a woman doesn't wear a veil, the man is responsible for his inability to control himself. As a married man I am also responsible for my wife in that I am given the duty of guiding her and my children, educating them in Islamic practices and guiding them along a path that leads to increased spirituality or building a stronger relationship with Allah.

Being from the West, where we're exposed to so much sex and lewdness, in coming to Islam one has to struggle hard not to be distracted from the path of Islam. Living in America it's very difficult with women liking you and liking you even more so because you're a Muslim. Non–Muslim women find a Muslim the ideal man because they know where he's going to be at night. They know he's not running around with some other woman, they know he's not in a bar drinking, he's not going to bring AIDS home. They view Muslims as good husbands and good fathers. Especially in the African–American communities in that the African–American community has been ripped apart, in that the man has been taken away from the household. She's looking for stability and certainty so she'd much rather be with a Muslim man even though he has two or three other wives. We say in America every man wants a Muslim woman, every woman wants a Muslim man. The nature of a man is to be inclined towards a woman who protects herself from being harassed and molested by other men, who doesn't freely show herself off and flaunt her beauty to other men. He wants his wife to be chaste. The nature of a woman is that she wants her husband to do the same. To be with her, to let her know that she is desirable, that they can build a relationship together. When I became a Muslim I was also starting university and you know a lot of women found it very interesting: Wow, you're a Muslim! The impression is that they're good husbands and good fathers. They're seen to be on a higher plane.

13 NAIMAH

"It's my duty," was the emphatic and cheerful reply when I phoned Naimah to ask her if she would like to talk to about her conversion to Islam and her life in Sudan. She invited me to visit her in Erkoweit, one of the smarter suburbs of Khartoum, where she lodged with a Sudanese family.

I went the next day. A lithe and vigorous black woman in her 50s wearing trousers and a waist–length hijab ushered me into a small single–storey villa. We settled down in a room furnished with angaraibs and little tables.

Naimah came to live in Sudan in 1998 with three of her adult children – an autistic son and two daughters – and has been there ever since apart from two years when they all went off to China to earn money to finance their plans for setting up a home and a school in Sudan.

Naimah epitomises the American "can do" spirit but she gives credit to Allah for everything that is done in her life and peppers her speech with constant expressions of gratitude to him. She is warm, dynamic, funny and idiosyncratic but sees herself modestly: "I'm like wallpaper. I'm just here."

I grew up in Los Angeles, California, and my family was a good Christian family. My mother was one of the best, bless her soul, and also my father. I have one sister and two brothers. We were Baptists, I went to church every Sunday, I sang in the choir from as early as I can remember, maybe 3 or 4 years old.

I had a very happy childhood. My mother was a very nurturing mother and sacrificing. We missed nothing. I found out later we were relatively poor but my stomach never felt it, I didn't realise it by my clothes.

I never for a moment questioned our religion. My focus on religion became stronger when I went into college and I took a class on comparative religion. This was a course I took for philosophy and this is when I found out about Islam.

All my life I was focused towards religion, through my family you know. I went into college at 17. Also I met my first husband when I was 16 and we married when I was 17 so everything came at the same time. He was about three years older.

There were other things going on at the time also. I had joined the Black Panther party and all the things that the teenagers were doing at that time I was doing all of it. This was in the 60's. But I'm not the sort of person who likes to be contained by an ideology. It was more just the practical thing. My girlfriend said to me: "Hey girl, there's this food distribution programme. Why don't you come along?" So I went along.

Later a friend of mine came over, my very best friend, she said "Oh, girl, come go with me, there's a group called the Nation of Islam and they have a lot of good–looking men over there." I said, "Really?" (I was divorced by this time.) She said "Yes, come go with me." I said "Yes, OK." But she said you have to wear a long dress and cover your hair and I said no problem. And so I put on the scarf and the long dress and I went with her and when I got there I said, oh, they're just men, what's the big deal? Her description was like there were these awesome, gorgeous, you know, men that were going to be just, you know, that you would just die for.

At that point she had probably been going a month or so and had become affiliated with the mosque there so I thought I might as well pay attention to what the man is going to be talking about and I began to listen. And what I will always remember was what the *imam* said with regards to Allah and his real strong push for the African–American to go back to school and to educate themselves and to contribute to the African–American community.

I was so moved by this lecture that the next day – I not only accepted Islam that night, the next day I went out and I enrolled, because I'd dropped out of college, I went back and enrolled in college, from then on it was a good life, it was Islam.

I did everything I was supposed to do as a member: take care of my family, learn to cook, learn how to sew. The women were really taught how to be good mothers and wives.

My mother was very happy because there was a period of my youth when I was going to parties and singing and doing things that of course my mother would not want me to do, no sane mother would want. So she was very happy. In fact, neighbours approached her and said we heard your daughter's a Muslim. She said yes, I'm very glad, I'm very happy. That stopped all of the gossip.

In 1975 Naimah broke with the Nation of Islam and became an orthodox Muslim. Shortly after that she got married again, to a Coptic Christian from Ethiopia.

Religion was no problem to him but it became a problem in the marriage I would say because at the time I was trying to raise the children to be Muslim, teaching them all of the *you can do, you cannot do* and of course they saw papa do something that they were taught a Muslim cannot do. This was confusing. So we talked about it, he and I, and made a mutual, adult decision to divorce. It was in the best interests of the children. But they remain close to their father and every year I would take the girls to be with him and his wife for the summer so there has never been a discontinuation between them and their father.

A year after the divorce Naimah, now with five children, married for the third time.

In the Muslim religion, when there are single people everybody is pushing you to become married and at the time I was working on a project, we were having a cultural benefit fair at our mosque. You know, in the States the African–American traditions are still mixed in Islamic affairs. At the time we were having fundraisers for a school that we were building, an Islamic school, and I was part of the team and I was on the entertainment committee and I was working with another group of Muslims who were also entertainers and we wrote songs, spiritually motivating songs, to encourage people to Islam and to get motivated. One of the brothers that was also singing in this group was the brother that I married. Someone gave me information that brother Hatim was interested in me and I gave feedback that, yes, I'm interested, and we got together – but never alone, no, in company – and in about two or three months we were married.

We moved out into the desert in 81 or 82. This move was *hijra*, oh yes, my move was *hijra*. I couldn't financially move to a Muslim country. I knew that I wanted to move my daughters and sons out of the city, away from the city life of partying and kids running up and down the streets and having lots of free time and dating and those kinds of concepts that were very prevalent in the years of my children growing up. So I didn't want them exposed to that. I didn't want them to ask me why can my neighbour watch TV when we get home from school all day and all night and we can't? Because I didn't allow my children to watch television. So to live the kind of life and provide the kind of environment that I wanted for my children I knew that it would be easier if I left the city and so we did. We looked around, we searched many areas, for just land and open space, travelling around in our car. We just piled up everything we thought was necessary along with the kids and took off looking for our dream *hijra* place.

Well, the car broke down, we had all kinds of crazy events, trials and tribulations. So since we had so many difficulties on the road, especially with the car, we returned back to the city and stayed three weeks while we were getting the car fixed with my mother and some friends. During that period of regrouping my husband had gone to the mosque one Friday and he came back and he said: guess what, there's a sheikh that is selling land to Muslims out in the desert and he's wanting to start a community for any Muslims that want to come. His name was Sheikh Azri, may Allah bless his soul, he passed away three years ago. He was Lebanese. So we went and visited the Sheikh and he took us to the desert and showed us this vast open dry land and I saw it and I said *alhamdulillah*, it's beautiful. So we moved there, we bought a sleep–six. Actually we went there with our car and a tent at first. After about a week – I had saved up money to get a sleep–six trailer – we moved into that trailer and over the course of a year we had added on a little building to the trailer and a little yard for chickens and we just began to expand. But of all the things that really went up there, the most useful and the thing that's still standing is the girls' playhouse. Hatim built them a playhouse out of scrap wood in the desert and that's where we had our school, inside their playhouse.

We were the first family to move to this particular community project. Others came about a year later. We had a mosque built in the desert about seven years later and we had Islamic services in a house in the city. It was a very nice life. It allowed me the seclusion and the freedom to home–school my children without interference. During the very hot times of day I would take the girls out to the library, we would have class in the library. At two o'clock we'd go shopping. And then at 4 or 5 we'd come home, when the sun was not so hot. So we set up our own schedule for dealing with the elements in the desert. It was a very good preparation for Sudan.

I divorced from brother Hatim in 91 or 92. The girls and I stayed in the desert another four years, just alone. It was safe, no problem, but it was wearing and tearing. We were running in and out from the desert to the college which was about 20 miles away so round about the thirteenth or fourteenth year I had to take an apartment near the college so the girls could go to the college by foot or by bus. But we still kept our home in the desert.

Throughout the whole time I was living in the desert I was

always planning *hijra* out of the country, asking Allah to give me a way, the money, the means, to get the girls out of the country. I was also a strong advocate of *hijra*. Many people, many families were coming to me asking how do you get the girls to be the way they are? They dress in the *niqab*, they don't give you problems, they're very responsible, how did you do it? I told them: I made *hijra*. You see, the first *hijra* I made was to the desert. I didn't allow any influence from the non–Muslim children, from my family. I would visit my family, my sister, and of course I would also monitor whatever activities were going on in the home with my sister and her children or whatever. I was only waiting for the girls to finish their college degree, then I would get them out because I didn't want them to marry in the States and have children there in that environment.

My main concern of course was having grandchildren grow up in America and then repeating the same kind of typical African–American experience of being discriminated against just because of colour. The problem is not direct and in your face, it's written in the books and in the laws and it's behind the doors. It's there. No one came and banged on my door, shot at my windows or burned crosses in front of my yard. But racism is real and any black American, especially any black American male that has tried to take any strong leadership position has been annihilated in America. The only ones that don't get annihilated are Colin Powell type of people.

I really began to focus on *hijra* as the girls were growing up, and I was seeing them getting older and I was thinking about marriage prospects for them and looking around and thinking, mm mm, not here and I then began to talk about *hijra* a lot in women's circles, the African–American Muslim women's circles, and began to also to prepare myself.

I was very novice in the idea. I had only travelled to Jamaica, so travelling out of the country was really something very new and I had no sense about what it was going to take to do all of it. I just went on a whim of 'I had to do it'. Of course, I was every

Ramadan reading Koran. So that inspired me. Koran inspired me to talk about it and to just seek ways and means to do it, work towards it. So during all these series of meetings – and I was with a very active women's group – I met a Muslim brother, a Sudanese Muslim brother, who heard me speaking in a group we had once, a marriage and family group session. He heard me speak about *hijra* and how it had been necessary for the continuance of the evolution of our families. He offered to let me meet his family here in Sudan and help me come here to just take a look. He advised, just go for a month. Don't take your family over there, go for a month, see if it's something you can adjust to, your girls can adjust to, and then make a decision. And so another friend of mine, another Muslim sister, she and I did just that, planned for six months, got a second job to get the money to come for a month here. After being here a month, visiting many places in Sudan, many Islamic conferences – there were lots of Islamic conferences and debates and this and that going on, some in Arabic and some in English, and we were taken to both, we were just taken around. He had told his friends, just take her everywhere and let her see all of Sudan, what it's like and we did just that and when I went back I was even more determined to work hard to make the money to make *hijra*. And since we had made some connection here, this is where we came to. When I was originally looking around I wanted to go to a Muslim country where the head of state is black so that in the future the children from my family, the boys, the male children, can aspire to become a leader or a president. He doesn't have to view his colour as an obstacle. So that was the main reason my thumbs went up when I came to Sudan. Oh, black president, black minister of foreign, you know, black this, black that, oh, yes. But also just the environment, you know, everywhere you look the women are dressed in *hijab*.

Two years later Naimah moved to Sudan with her three daughters, her autistic son, Naim, and her 'guardian child', the daughter of

*Muslim friends in the US who were also planning to make hijra
but could only afford to send one member of the family at the
time. By the time they arrived Sudanese friends had arranged
accommodation for them in Khartoum. Naimah and the girls
taught and worked on an educational programme that Naimah
had developed while working as a social worker in America.*

The familyship programme is geared towards dream–building.
A child's dream. Since I worked with at–risk kids, so called, I
wanted to give them another view of themselves and the best
way to approach a child, or any human being, to give assistance,
is to help them through what is interesting to them, through what
they feel they want to do, not what you think they should do.

I said to the other social workers, "You take my angels and I'll
take your monsters."

It started with these kids, the monsters. I used my own children
as role models, as peer tutors for the kids.

So this is where I came up with the dream–building approach.
We developed a kind of dream assessment for children to find out
what their ideas and feelings were about themselves and towards
their future. What they thought could help them become what
they wanted to become. I developed an independent study for
each child based on what they were interested in.

I could say it started with my own kids because that was my
philosophy in home–schooling. I didn't want a school or a teacher
in a public school to tell my child, oh you don't want to be that,
you don't want to look like this, you don't want to be a rock
digger, you want to be a doctor. I didn't want that. I wanted them
to develop their own sense of identity and self–worth through
Islamic traditions and ways and means. So the familyship was
a carryover from raising and educating my daughters to this
programme with the children.

For the programme I created to bring us all together as a family,
I required the parents to bring the children to the agency for an
additional one day a week so they could all come together and

we had a four–hour long programme. Then after three months we added on a Saturday and Sunday. At first the foster parents grumbled but after they began to see the change in the children's behaviour they were more than happy to drop them off. And this became my charity work, this Saturday and Sunday.

The Islamic lifestyle concept was there but nothing taught, only modelled. What we taught was etiquettes, charity, you know, through modelling, taking them out to give food and saying to them, do you remember when you were hungry, did you ever think oh I wish somebody would do this, this, this? Let's fulfil someone's dream today, let's go out and give food to poor people.

The familyship programme took on the name because I was using my family as the treatment vehicle for the children. As the curriculum developed we took the concept of familyship into the charter school programme. I became a facilitator and director for the Muslim children in the programme. We made our home a home–school, a satellite school, for Muslim children. Our school was residential, they stayed in our home for four days a week and went home for three days.

In Sudan I could focus less on having to work to pay for meals. So it gave me more time to focus on doing the kind of thing I like to do in the line of humanitarian work. Because we took children from, you know the ones who come and knock on the door and beg or try to steal. We took these children into our home and set up a programme for them. We didn't go out looking for anybody. Allah sent them to my doorstep. So you just, as a Muslim, it's your duty, your obligation.

Naimah plans to set up home–schools in places outside Khartoum and has already bought land in a small village called Tisain and also in Maierno, where Mohammed Abdul Qaadir intends to establish a khalwa with a group of other Western converts.

Someone would say, hey, I know somebody, or I know a sheikh

that has land and they would love to have this kind of thing that you want to do. Just like that. Just word of mouth. With Tisain I met some friends of people that I knew. We were eating somewhere, maybe it was during Ramadan, and you know how the ladies sit and talk, and they said, oh Naimah wants to have a home–school for little girls and this and this, and someone who was sitting there said oh, I know a sheikh in Tisain who dada dada dada, would you like to meet him and that sort of thing.

They use sheikh for an older man who's respected. They use sheikh for a learned man who teaches. Really he's just a nice person. We went to visit and he showed me around their farmland and projects. He'd just bought a cow or something like that and they were planning to do something with cows, maybe in the future breed them. The projects are just on a village level, but it was nice. I'm a country bumpkin so to me it's like, wow! To someone else it would be oh, why do you want to be here? But I just loved it. It was nice and spacious and green. To see greenery in Sudan it's just really nice. I met his wife and children. It was just a regular kind of introduction. And the houses are the usual, made of mud bricks, with a *hosh*. They have electricity and they have running water.

I hope that, *inshallah*, for the pleasure of Allah, I can, wherever I am, make a place for children. If by the time I'm there and it's built Allah sends children knocking on my door, it's going to be for those kids. If I get a call saying, oh Naimah, take my daughter, or the girls, it's going to be for those kids. I don't have a restriction on who can come or who cannot come. And you know, in a Muslim home you teach Islam, you practise Islam. And you also teach the required academics. You teach the homemaking skills. You teach girls how to become women, how to become mothers, good mothers.

I've met the sheikh in Maierno too. But in Islam the men and women don't sit together and spend lots of time together. I had a meeting with him, we had a couple of meetings, just targeted towards my own interests in terms of Maierno but to just sit around, no. While I was there I was entertained by the female family of the sheikh.

Whenever I get something built out there I'll go. It depends on, you know in America you can make plans and say I'm planning to do something on this day. But in Third World countries it doesn't go that way. So I don't frustrate myself in the way I used to in trying to make plans and then find out that you can't do it because of, you know, something dumb. But now I'm more focused on taking things a day at a time. You need some money going in so that you don't have to work or find a way to make money while you're living in that area, because they're poor so you're going to work for who, in those areas? They need help from you. So to build a home where we don't have to worry about paying rent and to make our home energy self–sufficient, solar energy, and that sort of thing, it's going to take money. This is our focus now.

Naimah's claim to be anti social seems inconsistent with a desire to live in Sudan where neighbourliness and social obligations are so fundamental to daily life, particularly in the kind of village which she plans to live in.

I'm an African–American. I'm not Sudanese. I spend a lot of time with myself and my daughters, with the family in this house, and I have another very good friend, a Sudanese lady who lives in Erkoweit. I visit her maybe once every two weeks or so or she comes to me. I will attend any gathering of women that is focused towards education and Islam, focused towards learning and study. But social things like sitting around sharing tea, talk and this kind of thing, I don't do that in America, it's just not me. I'm not a socialiser. I'm like wallpaper. I'm just here.

I don't plan to change my lifestyle; my lifestyle is really simple. If I have to work, I get up, I shower, say my prayers, read Koran, go to work, come home, pray, eat and then relax and do what I want to do. Now that's my lifestyle. If someone comes over, or calls, I hear what's going on, what they want to talk about,

I deal with the conversation, and then do what I want to do. If my daughters want me to do something, or I want them to do something, or we have something planned, we do that. That's my lifestyle. I don't plan for that to change.

Naimah's two younger daughters are still unmarried but she expects that this will soon change.

That's always open. We don't have a mate selected but that's my agenda for them. It's as Allah wills. If I see someone I think is suitable and I do a background check and find that he is I'll suggest that they take a look. If they find someone, if Allah sends someone in their environment, like I have one girl that's going to be working at the BEI school, well maybe Allah will put someone in that environment. If that happens and she comes to me and says I'm interested, what do you think, we'll do a background check on him. It will be as Allah decrees, however Allah decrees. I'm not the master of the universe. Allah will make a way for them. Allah will make a way and will make it easy.

14 ZARINA

*The mud–brick room measures about 3 metres by 3 metres. Inside,
under a sapling and thatch roof, it is whitewashed. A thin layer of
mottled grey lino covers the floor and a grey curtain with a pattern
of crossed daggers and palm trees hangs across the back wall. A
bunch of plastic flowers stands on a small low table beside a pile of
books: The Human Genome, How the Brain Works, Dealing with
Children. There are two metal armchairs, a wardrobe, a floor fan,
a couple of stools and a single metal bed, designed by Zarina and
made by the local blacksmith. It is shaped like a chaise longue with
a curving curlicued frame along the back and top. The room is in
Kalakla, a small town not far from Khartoum.*

*Zarina Davis, a British–Caribbean woman, has been living in
Sudan for four years and has converted to Islam twice. She sits on
the chaise longue as she talks.*

I was born in 1971 in Peterborough, Cambridgeshire. I had four
sisters and two brothers. One sister and one brother were half
because my father used to live with another woman before he
married my mum. I went to the the Lindons Junior School and
after that to the Ken Simpson School which used to be the county
grammar school.

There were lots of Asians at school, more than white people.
There were quite a few West Indians as well but not as many as
Asians. I liked Asians and I was highly influenced by them. Hence
the name Zarina. My original name was Susan Jane. I changed it
to Zarina in 1990. I think it's Afghani or Iranian. I chose it because
when I was little I used to like Sabrina from Charlie's Angels

because she was the thinnest one and the darkest one, the one I could identify with because she was different from the other girls.

Our family were churchgoers. At that time we went to the Church of God Seventh Day. It was a Church of God group. It's a gospel church, the ones that clap hands and get the spirit. Black people go. At first I enjoyed it and then I saw that the church didn't reflect reality. I mean, when you're little you wanted it to because it was a lovely thing but when you go out to the real world.... When you went to the baptisms and the conventions and things it was all a show, everyone looking nice but in reality the majority of these people were struggling and didn't have enough money and most of them weren't properly educated.

My father got made redundant in 1981 or 82. It was the year when everybody started to go back to the West Indies, because there were loads of redundancies and a lot of people started to go back. We went back to Jamaica in 1982.

I enjoyed it. We stayed there for nine and a half months. I even went to school there.

Then the big thing that affected my life was that when I went back to England, where before I'd enjoyed myself with my friends at Ken Simpson School, when I went back I was on the outside of that relationship. We used to go round as three, when I went back they were just going round as two. Things had all changed. I had expected that I would go back and take my place among my friends but they turned round and they hated me. In the end, before I left they invited me back but I lost so many years. So when I went to other schools and other places after that I had problems getting on with other people.

I left school in 1987. I went to Peterborough regional college and did a diploma in travel and tourism because I wanted to travel. Then I wanted to move to Birmingham so I did a travel course in Birmingham.

I converted to Islam when I was 17 in Birmingham. I converted because I wanted to be secure and clean, to have a secure family in the end. I wanted to get married, stay married, have a family and have a community which was not Western, a community where even if anything went wrong you wouldn't get dumped, you wouldn't get abandoned. A community where you could be different, where no one was pressing you to be a certain way like how some of my family did because I wasn't quick like them. Remember, I had problems coming from childhood because I was a bit slower when I was younger so I felt different and bad, I felt self–hatred and lack of confidence. It made my ability to learn and to do jobs and to keep jobs and to provide for my needs and to interact and adapt with people and all sorts of things – it messed up all of that.

At this stage converting to Islam did not bring any of the positive personal results that Zarina had been hoping for.

To diminish those feelings you need to know how to apply the parts of the Koran, like applying the thought style and the priority of thoughts, and thought patterns. And I didn't know all that. It was after that that I found out about NLP. I was in Birmingham and there's a cultural centre where they did dance classes and exercises and stuff. I saw this poster talking about self–mastery, how to get the results you want or something like this, and it had NLP. There was a man there and I started firing him with questions. I went to this seminar thing where they were talking about it and practising some parts of it. I got addicted to it. I had private sessions with an NLP practitioner, about how I could resolve some of my anger, why I couldn't do things, why I couldn't do jobs, why I couldn't learn quickly, why I wasn't confident. He really dug some stuff out. It was all the top layer. But now I've got right down to the bottom layer stuff. Now I know what to do because I've got experience. It's just reprogramming the mind. That's all it is. You reprogramme the mind so your mind and body know what to do in different situations, and the sort of thoughts to think, then you find yourself not using old childish behaviours. From that time I've been working on it till now, getting down to the real basic feelings that you had when you were a baby. I felt that my mother and my family were a bit too hard and I didn't have the ability to adapt.

After converting to Islam Zarina was forced to recant by her family.

I have some family, like my uncle – we call them the Famous Five, because it's my father's brother, my father's sister and their husband and wife and a daughter – they go round together. They start preaching and saying "In the name of Jesus, the devil…" and they go on and on about demons and they say that you've got the devil in you. Anyway, they sat me in a van for about three hours and they made me do it. They made me change back to Christianity by force. They sat me in the van – all of them were there – and they pressure you to do what they say.

They used to drive round the whole of England preaching and one time my sister, when she'd just moved into a new house, her new neighbour came and she was pregnant and the people just came to the house all of a sudden without phoning or anything and they said, "Oh you've got a blue baby, you've got a blue baby." My sister's neighbour, she was so scared I think she went white and they're telling her she's got a blue baby. "In the name of Jesus," they said, and they started pouring water and they were rubbing her. They reckoned that the Holy Spirit was giving them messages.

Zarina got married to a Tunisian Muslim in 1990 and had a daughter in the same year but the marriage did not work out.

I got involved with Tunisia because I went with the Solihull College in 1988 as part of the diploma course. I fell in love with Tunisia, and I went back there on my own and met my husband there. Then I had a daughter.

She never lived with us because we didn't have proper accommodation and we didn't have enough money to live properly. And I realised he married me to go to England and because he had money problems. When I had her I went back to England to finish off a course, the national diploma course. Remember that at the time there was a recession. I had no skills. You need skills to work so you can make yourself comfortable and be secure. He was a painter and he couldn't hold down a job. He'd always argue with the people over money.

When I went back to Tunisia from England he put me in a hotel. The house he was in with his brothers was broken down and dirty. The bed was broken. He didn't have a cupboard or a mattress or anything. There was no toilet or shower. He wasn't working.

I stayed for two years. I went to work. As far as I was concerned, I was married to the man. You've got to work and sort it out. That was how I thought. But I saw this man was not wanting to help me sort things out. He wanted to go to Britain. And my sisters, when I went back to England, they said how come you didn't notice, how come you couldn't tell that that was what he wanted. I thought, that's strange, why are they asking me that. I wasn't even aware of that. I told you that I was damaged from when I was young because I was slower than other people so people thought I was stupid. So I hated myself and I didn't discover or develop the thinking strategies and all those things that other teenagers were developing. I didn't develop them because I stopped. I remember that Ken Simpson thing when I got back from Jamaica and I was left on the outside. And it caused me a lot of emotional problems: self–control, controlling your body, making yourself do things, getting your mind to do what you want it to do, knowing what to say to people, I couldn't work it out, I always got it wrong, and I was always being very emotional and very angry and frustrated about things because I couldn't get the result I wanted.

In the end I started having these daydreams, and the daydreams are the things that tell you what's really happening. Any time you get a daydream don't see it as just a load of rubbish. It's telling you something, because it's your real feelings coming out. The daydream was of this character and the character had a real bad temper problem and had a bad family history but he was a high performer, etc., everything that my husband was not. My character had lots of my sister in him because I had problems with my sister. She was older than me and quicker than me and she didn't accept me because she thought that I took her place and she was jealous of me. So she punished me for being in her place, she used to say that I was stupid. So this character was the opposite of this even though a lot of his personality came from her. There was a lot of violence in those stories. I worked out that it meant emotional violence because people were rejecting me all the time and emotionally blocking me out. This is the same as taking someone and throwing them on the floor.

When the child was first born I was glad that the family took responsibility so that I could go back to England and not end up on income support struggling with a baby like a single parent when I had a husband. So I let the family look after the child.

I wasn't close to the baby in the beginning because when I had her I went back to England to finish off the diploma. When I had her I wasn't so keen on having a baby because I had no proper accommodation for myself, no proper job or income and my husband wasn't close to me. I had wanted a baby with my husband around and a proper income. And I wanted to feel complete in myself, I mean psychologically and educationally. Then I could have a baby because I'd feel I'd got enough to give then. Later I was used to the fact that she wasn't there.

The last two years in Tunisia, there were a lot of problems because he was renting a broken–down place. First he was in the Medina and I said we're going to move because I didn't want these men sitting in the house all the time and me living in that room like a person from out of nowhere. There wasn't a proper toilet or shower, there wasn't anything. In the end we went to another place. His mother forced him to rent a proper place and everything was a bit better. But there was too much arguing and fighting over money. I was working but they weren't paying enough. The man was really exploiting me. I was working as an import–export secretary and he used to pay me just 150 Tunisian dinars which is 150 dollars a month.

So I went back to England and I started upgrading myself. At that time I had no proper work experience in the office. I went straight in at the deep end, struggling to earn a salary to provide for myself and study. Because I couldn't do maths properly I didn't go on conventional courses, I did all this NVQ stuff. I did the programming one. It was beneficial because it proved that I could do programming. Even though there was stuff I didn't understand something in me knew that if I carried on I would understand it and then I can do it. But I was always still not satisfied so in the end, just before I came to Sudan, just before my money ran out, I did a Kumon course to tackle this maths problem thing because I wanted to get over it. So I can do what I want to do now without hindrance or being held back. I was weak at maths because no one had the ability to help me understand but I find when I'm here in Sudan, a Sudanese sits with you and helps you to understand and you understand him and that's it.

I got back to the UK at the end of 1993. I had married in 1990, came back to the UK, finished the course, had the recession. After that I was just unemployed in Britain. My parents got the money together and sent me back to Tunisia. They said you should be with your husband and child, which is right, but who wants to take a child to live with them when they're not secure. If you're going to have a baby you want security. You can't be having a baby and you're not feeling secure. And then when you're feeling yourself to be not adequate you don't want to be bothered by anything or anyone, you just want to complete your development. For a start, do the studies and get the work you want. Get money in hand and feel OK about yourself and then afterwards you can think about a baby.

Zarina went back to Tunisia and got divorced in 1998. The following year she went to Sudan as a volunteer English teacher.

I came here with the Sudan Volunteer Programme. They sent me to Omdurman. I taught in Ahfad University. Then after that I said to one of the managers I wanted to study Arabic. He arranged for me to go to the African University. My Arabic's not so brilliant but I can communicate, that's the important thing. I can read and write it but with mistakes.

I wanted to learn Arabic when I came here. If I learned Arabic then I could get the Islamic books and the stuff I wanted and read up what I wanted to read. I wanted Arabic because I love it, and because of the connection with Islam and the culture and the people. I was always drawn to Islam and the Sufis, the mystical Islam and the scientific aspects that can be applied. It's not just the religion I wanted, it's the people I'm interested in. Some people go just for the religion and are not interested in the people which I think is empty. It's the people that make the religion and the religion makes the people. You see religion is there for the people and not people just for the religion. The religion is a system. The religion is there to develop something, to culture something. It's there to culture the people. So it's the people I'm interested in.

I learned a lot at the African University. They did an Arabic course where they taught you lots of Islamia. I found that my Arabic was very weak at that time and it still isn't strong now. Someone is going to have to study the Arabic language for three or four years to learn it properly before they can get the hang of dealing with Islamic subjects. Actually Islam is quite philosophical. It's not what you see on television about men bossing women about and terrorists and all that you get on the news. It's a peaceful religion. It's about solving problems. There was a book that we had, we called it *qra'a*, for reading and comprehension. It dealt with a lot of life's problems and how they should be dealt with in an Islamic way. Actually solutions are being applied today in the West under different names like NLP, different Western scientific names, but they've been there in Islam longer than I would ever know because a lot of those stories have been taught from generation to generation through the Muslim community and yet I got some of this stuff or came across it in other Western materials under totally different names. The same principle. A lot of things like NLP have been in Islam for a long time. I tend to pick out its problem solving properties because I still have problems to solve. About women and men, if you marry properly it creates a secure situation. Any human has a right to cling to another human. That is his own territory. That means your parents, or your siblings and your wife, your partner, and your kids. You should be able to do this. It should not be like in the West where you feel that you can't do that.

Living conditions in the students' residence at the African University were less satisfactory.

I lived at the *dakhlia* for a short time and then I left. I was sharing a room with four other people, Sudanese and other Africans. It was very dirty and noisy. After that I was living at the centre behind the African University. It was also dirty but the conditions were better. The food was still bad. I was still sharing a room, but it was more comfortable, and the people were nicer.

I made the *shahada* in February 2001. I met this woman at Sheikh Al Burai's mosque. I got friendly with her, I was looking for a place to stay and I spoke to her and she offered me somewhere. She was the one that took me to the court in Omdurman. They just took us straight in and it was a woman judge that day. She was quite a tough one and she was crying and the witnesses were crying and the woman – my friend – she was crying. I didn't know the witnesses, they were just people standing around the courts. They were happy to witness; they get extra points. When they went home they would have had a good story to tell their friends. We went to a shop across the road and got some sweets and offered them to the security guards who ate them all and hardly anybody else got any.

The big change was that I was praying by that time. Well, I started praying before I made the *shahada* because I thought I'd take it slowly because I was so damaged by that experience with my family in the van. I went back to Islam slowly.

Zarina belongs to one of the Sufi sects, the Sammaniya, and follows Sheikh Al Burai who is well known in Sudan both as a leading Sufi and as a writer of religious poems and songs. She learned about the sheikh through a man who was trying to persuade her to enter into a secret marriage with him.

A secret marriage is where you marry in secret and then you can divorce, or the man just treats the woman badly or does what he wants with her. Anyway, I went to see Sheikh Al Burai in a place called Zariba, in the countryside. There they have a *khalwa*, where people learn the Koran. They even have mad people who go there. They have a place where mad people are locked up and they read the Koran to them and do other readings and give them special medicines. They put verses of the Koran near them or write it or put it on them and so they wear it like a necklace or on their arm or something, or soak it in water and then they drink the water until the devil gets out.

If you've got any problem he can solve it. He can make a prayer for you or he can give you some *buhur*, which is some incense which you burn and inhale. Then he can give you some paper which you can also burn or drink, you leave it to soak and then drink the water. It's written with Koran. Another thing is he can touch you and pray.

You know in England you've got New Age people and traditional healers. I've been to reiki. It's like reiki. When you get raiki you feel different. When you visit Sheikh Al Burai you feel the difference. Now one time I was feeling sad and not OK and I said everything to him that I felt and he touched me once or twice on my head and all of that just went. He knows what he's doing. He's working with your electromagnetic field. So when you go there you won't see anything strange happening but what you will feel, you'll feel the difference. And even when you look around you things feel brighter and more alive there. You're in a natural setting and no pollution and then the people, they're coming there with all their hopes and dreams and they're getting them met. Throughout the year they come but when it's Eid time, there are bus-loads. They're travelling at three o'clock in the morning. If he didn't have an effect on anyone, no one would go back, would they? It's like his music. It's religious but it's not like this *Ansar al Sunna (makes a series of whooping noises to illustrate her point)*. It's soft, loving and relaxing. Islam should be something soft, loving, relaxing and flexible. Something where you sit down and relax with your friends and family, you drink your tea or whatever. It shouldn't be something *(makes whooping noise again)*.

I went to see Sheikh Al Burai because I had some accommodation problems and I wanted to be married and wanted to sort out money problems and I needed to learn the Arabic language.

I passed my Arabic diploma in the end. Everything takes time. You have to pursue a problem, not just see the sheikh and sit down. You see the sheikh and go back to your work and carry on working at it.

I stayed for about six weeks the first time I went. I stayed in – you know those huts that belong to the Western Arabs. Jawaama, that's the name of the tribe. The huts are made out of *ghash*. It's not just grass, they're hard, not straw, they're bushes, they're actually bushes, you know, branches, but they're not just any branches, they're straight. They look grassy when you're far away but when you get near you see that it's a thick type of thing. It's cool inside and when it rains you don't get wet inside.

It was sandy, and you could see the watermelons were so big and sweet and the trees were plenty but yet everything was white sand. It was winter. When you looked at it, it was like the rolling hills of England. Just beautiful. And the water is so clear and clean and fresh. When you wash your hair your hair goes silky, like silk wool.

That time it was during Ramadan when I went so I'd get up, fast, eat at night, pray, sleep again. I'd read to prepare myself because I had exams coming. And then after reading I'd sit down with the Koran to try and get my tongue round the Arabic and I used to talk to the women in the house about my problems. I was staying in someone's house. They were *Sammaniya*. They had their own local sheikh in their family there. Sheikh Al Burai is for the whole of Sudan. There are people outside of Sudan now who take *tariqa* from Sheikh Al Burai.

This was in the village of Amdam. Sheikh Al Burai is in Zariba, about twenty to thirty minutes away. The first place I stayed in was Sheikh Al Burai's wife's house and his daughter was there. I didn't recognise that I was in the house of Sheikh Al Burai himself. I didn't know this until about a year later.

When you're in the countryside you don't need much. You just need some cotton and soap and something to oil your hair and skin with. These are the important things. You have to be clean; you can't go filthy just because you're in the countryside.

Zarina spent six weeks in Kordofan. When she returned to Khartoum she started working at a language school in Kalakla.

I had money problems so I got a job with BEI and they moved me to Kalakla. BEI found me somewhere to stay. I was staying with a family. The first family I was with was an Arab family. They were lovely people but their kids were naughty. The kids ran wild, they didn't listen. And I'm a person who likes to relax, I like to have my own way, my own room with no one interested. I'll just go to my room and sit down and do my work and sleep or whatever. I'm not talkative in the house. Then they wanted their room back. The house was too small. At that time I'd made friends with the cleaner at BEI, and that cleaner she's from the south of Sudan, she's not Arab, she's African. She's Fujillu and her husband's Dinka but he's dead now. I'm living in their house, I rent this room from them. There's the mother, a daughter and four sons. They're quite free and relaxed. Yes, they're Muslim and everything. Oh yes, you've got southern Muslims. I pay 100,000 pounds a month for the room, electricity and water.

When I came here the room was bad. I had cement put on the floor, I had the walls painted and I furnished it. They had no shower room and no proper toilet. So they dug a pit – you know the countryside toilet, the one where they dig a pit – and they built a washroom. It's very basic. It's just cement walls and just something to cover the top and you can have a shower there. You just go inside and you take your bucket. Well, I've got a big water barrel there. I've got my barrel inside so they fill it up in the evening when the water pressure's high. I bought a long hose and so they just fill up the water and when you want to go and take a shower or wash your hair the water's there. In the main rooms they had electricity but in the other rooms that they used to let to different people they didn't have any electricity. I said to them if I move into this house the first thing you have to do, wire the electricity from your room there to my room. You just buy the wire and connect it. *Alhamdullila* they did.

I feel secure here because I know that there are people in the house that will look after your stuff. I know them and they know me and I trust them and they trust me. I can leave my room and lock it and no one's going to break in because someone's always in the house. When I'm in my room I read and do whatever I like to do. They don't normally disturb me because they know that, well, I'm like one of the family but I am a *hawaja* and, OK, I'm the same colour as they are but my language is different and my behaviour's going to be different so they're understanding.

For meals I normally eat at the places where I work because I'm working all day. At the weekend, because I work, *alhamdulila*, I can get some money out and then I buy them some meat or something nice – one of the boys'll run and get it, and they cook it and we have a big breakfast and everyone eats and relaxes and I just go back and fall asleep because I'm knackered by the end of the week.

Given the nature of Muslim society it might be assumed that a single woman would find it more difficult to integrate into Sudan than a single man.

I wanted to get married but I see a lot of opposition from families. They don't want the *hawaja* in. The thing is the people I wanted to marry, many of them were dishonest, they wanted to marry me in secret so as to play and not to be responsible. And one of them that was serious, his family agreed in the beginning and changed their mind at the end. It's not so important that the family agree because the family will disagree at first and they'll agree at the end but they were causing trouble, they wouldn't talk to him and things like that.

The house I live in I sit and I eat with them. I can visit any of those houses in Kalakla. In the evening I tend to go to my friends Michael and Sarra. We meet up in Amarat, we sit down. I take *sheesh*. Sometimes we sit at a café, we just relax.

As I left we walked across the hosh to the main room of the house to meet Zarina's landlady, Muna. She was watching a film on satellite television with some female neighbours. The men lay on angaraibs outside, under a rakuba. Zarina chatted to them in fluent Arabic. She seemed like one of the family.

15 SOUTH TO ZARIBA

Zarina's story about Sheikh Al Burai and Zariba had fascinated me. I decided to pay a visit.

Sheikh Al Burai is famous throughout Sudan. There was no shortage of people ready to give me advice on how to get there, or to offer personal introductions to the sheikh or his entourage.

"Take the bus to El Obeid and then you can get a minibus to Zariba," said one.

"No need for that," said another. "There's a bus that goes directly from Omdurman to Zariba every day."

"You don't want to do that," said a third. "The bus is one of these local ones, like a lorry. Very uncomfortable and off road all the way."

"I know the Sheikh's son, I'll call him for you," offered Ahmed Babiker.

"My grandfather, the *sheikha's* husband, can go with you," volunteered Nagla. "He's a *huwar* of Sheikh Al Burai."

"Kamal can go with you," Omar suggested. "He's very interested in Sheikh Al Burai."

Kamal was too busy to go but he rang me one Thursday morning to say that he had spoken with friends in El Obeid who knew the Sheikh. He insisted that I should go that very day as the next day was Friday, the day on which there would be most religious activity and the Sheikh most likely to be available. "Get an afternoon bus to El Obeid," he said, "and my friends will meet you at the bus station and take you to their house to spend the night. In the morning they'll put you on the bus for Zariba and arrange for someone to look after you. Phone me after you get to the bus station to tell me what time you'll be arriving and I'll let them know."

I threw a few things into a bag and went out to the bus station at Souk Shaabi. Sudan has, surprisingly, a number of bus companies which operate fleets of luxury coaches over a network of routes connecting the main destinations.

A chucker–in was already waiting when I opened the taxi door.

"Where to?"

"El Obeid,"

"This way, come with me." He hustled me off to the office of one of the bus companies.

After I'd bought my ticket I went to a phone booth to call Kamal. He was out of the office. I gave the person who answered the phone my arrival time and asked him to pass on the message. I hung up with the uneasy realisation that I didn't have a phone number for the people I was supposed to meet, nor did I know their names.

El Obeid, the capital of North Kordofan, lies about 500 kilometres south of Khartoum. As we bowled out of the city an attendant came round offering the passengers sweets from a glass basket filled with toffees. The driver put on a cassette of religious music, an unaccompanied androgynous voice with a sedately jolly bouncing sound. The attendant came round again with plastic cups and a jug of cold water. For the next seven hours we drove through vast tracts of desert and scrub. The religious music was soon replaced by the screaming and yelling of an Egyptian video with some very un–Islamic scenes: disco dancing, drinking, scantily dressed women and a man walking around a dress shop groping the breasts of dummies wearing bikinis. The attendant distributed lunch boxes containing fried chicken, olives, crumbly white cheese and a syrup–drenched cake.

As we travelled further south the cuboid style of the village houses began to give way to lopsided round huts with conical thatched roofs. In the late afternoon there was a prayer stop. Everyone got off, mats were unrolled, hands, feet and faces were washed using water from plastic jugs which seemed to appear from nowhere, and they all bowed down in unison towards Mecca.

At eight o'clock we arrived at El Obeid bus station. It was dark and there was a power cut. The other passengers dispersed and I sat waiting at the bus company office, a small booth lit by a single candle. The uneasy feeling I'd had in Khartoum started to grow.

Half an hour later a man sat down beside me. He introduced himself as Mubarak, the bus company manager and asked why I was sitting there.

"Some people are coming to meet me but they haven't arrived yet."

"Have you got a phone number for them?"

I had to admit that I didn't, and that I didn't even know who they were or where they lived.

"Do you know anyone else in El Obeid?"

I knew Ismat, a man who had worked for me in the past, but I hadn't been able to contact him as he had no phone.

"Do you know Ismat who works at the Sudanese–British Cultural Centre?" I asked, without the faintest hope that, in a city of about a quarter of a million inhabitants, he would do.

"Yes, I know Ismat. In fact, I know where he is right now. He's at the Al Mirikh Sports Club. I'll call the club on my mobile right away."

Within ten minutes Ismat was at the bus station.

Ismat is that rarity in Sudan, a good organiser. No sooner had I explained everything than he had matters in hand. We went to a hotel in the market area, a utilitarian East–European looking sort of structure where I was offered a room without breakfast for 10,000 dinars. "Forty US dollars," said the manager, thinking I might not be familiar with Sudanese money. I was horrified; not so much because it was outrageously expensive – which it was, for a room like a grey prison cell, with even the window panes covered in grey paint, and a shower and toilet in a kind of cupboard in the wall which you had to climb into – but because

I had so little money with me, having been counting on the hospitality of Kamal's friends in El Obeid and expecting to have very little to buy in Zariba. It left me no margin for any emergency that might crop up.

The next morning Ismat called for me at seven o'clock, having already bought me a ticket for a pickup truck going to Zariba.

While we waited for the truck to fill up we had breakfast crouching on stools under a tree, little glasses of coffee spiced with ginger and hot fried batter sprinkled with sugar.

For 500 dinars extra Ismat had managed to get me a seat in the cabin, squeezed between the driver and a large man who could easily have occupied the entire space himself. The back of the truck filled up with men and women jam–packed together. We rattled off and were soon out of El Obeid, weaving across the desert along a route traced out by the wheels of previous vehicles. The windscreen had been smashed into a crazy paving of cracks by flying stones. I peered through it at a terrain studded with bushes, thorn trees and baobabs. Boy shepherds tended small flocks of sheep, groups of aloof camels wandered about with stately gait. In the thatch villages women gathered at wells with buckets and jerrycans, old men jogged along on donkeys, boys kicked balls about.

After about an hour and a half the landscape changed, turning to pure desert with dunes and very little vegetation. After another hour and a half a minaret appeared in the distance, surrounded by an oasis of greenery. We had arrived at Zariba.

We all got out of the truck in a small market area where vendors sold fruit, vegetables, a few basic commodities and masses of pictures, trinkets and amulets associated with Sheikh Al Burai. Just beyond it lay the Sheikh's compound, dominated by a large green, white and grey mosque with three minarets soaring into the sky like Cape Canaveral rockets.

I got talking with the only other foreigner among the passengers, a Syrian called Rateb with a tousled and bleary–eyed look and a resemblance to Rasputin. His reasons for visiting Zariba were not clear. He seemed more interested in telling me about the water processing device which he worked on in Saudi Arabia and picking my brains about how he could market it in Europe.

Hundreds of people were crowding into the religious compound, most of them hoping for a personal meeting with the Sheikh who holds a regular Friday *majlis* in a kind of mansion inside the compound. Rateb wanted to talk with the Sheikh and suggested I go along with him.

The mansion was surrounded by railings with one gate controlled by three or four guards. Rateb and I joined the throng of people who were shoving and elbowing each other in an effort to get to the front. Now and again the guards would open the gate just a crack to let one or two people in and then slam it shut again to keep the rest out. More by the force of random pushing than anything else Rateb and I were propelled to the top of the queue. I didn't know what criteria the guards used in allowing admission but supposed that, as foreigners, we would probably be allowed in. We were, and just as the gate opened I felt myself seized from behind by three pairs of hands, the owners of which, sticking to me like barnacles to a ship's hull, were catapulted inside. Selma, Somaya and Amal started chattering to me as if we were old friends, took my hand, showed me where to put my shoes and indicated to the guards that we were all together. They had earmarked me as their passport to the Sheikh's presence.

Inside a vast pillared hall, carpeted and cushioned Arab–style, we joined about a hundred other people, most of them sitting on the floor. This, it turned out, was only the ante–chamber. Small groups of people were processed through another door from time to time and directed to the Sheikh in a room upstairs.

Selma, Somaya and Amal were thrilled to bits about having gained admission so easily. They all worked for Kenana Sugar Company in Gezira state and had travelled to Zariba in the hope of being able to see Sheikh Al Burai and ask for help with their personal problems. People sometimes have to wait weeks to see him, they told me. We were joined by three other women, all of whom wanted the Sheikh to help them find husbands. We settled down on the floor with handfuls of sticky dates and bottles of water chilled in an ice bucket. Rateb seemed delighted to find himself surrounded by so many women and was soon getting on like a house on fire with Somaya. He took a bottle of perfume out of his pocket and handed it round for us all to sprinkle ourselves.

From outside came the sound of drumming. I left the women inside and went out. A group of men playing drums, tambourines and cymbals were walking around, running in little spurts, backwards and forwards. Another, larger group formed a ring round them, chanting and swaying, moving in a kind of conga–like motion. Groups of women formed yet another ring on the outside, bopping and ululating. Many of the women were very casually dressed, some with short sleeves, some in trousers even, and very scanty *tarhas*. The atmosphere was more like that of a wedding or a party.

The call for Friday prayer started. I went back into the Sheikh's house. All the people inside were now hustling to get out as the Sheikh was expected to come down and go over to the mosque. There was an atmosphere of near hysteria as a frail, elderly man appeared, surrounded by a group of helpers. People pushed and shoved in an effort to catch a glimpse of him, to get near him. Those who did seized his hand, kissing it. A big white Land Rover waited to drive the Sheikh the couple of hundred yards to the mosque. Beside it stood a pickup truck with a group of soldiers manning a set of guns mounted in the back.

During the prayers Amal and I wandered out into the village. I was interested in the houses which, with their round thatch huts, were so different from what I was used to seeing further north. Amal knocked at a gate. "This *khawaja* wants to come in and have a look at your house," she said to the woman who opened it. "*Ahlan*," smiled the woman. "*Itfaddalu*."

Aisha showed us round the compound where she lived with her mother, her sister and two children of indeterminate parentage. The living space was mostly outside in a large *hosh*. Several *angaraibs* were grouped under an open–sided *rakuba*. The two round huts which completed the accommodation were windowless and served mainly as storage space for kitchen equipment and clothes. We sat in the *rakuba* to drink some water, thanked her and left.

Back at the mosque Amal took me into a square building surmounted by a beehive–shaped dome, painted with bands of pale and dark green. It was the tomb of Sheikh Al Burai's father. The bier stood in the middle of the room, covered with a black embroidered cover. People crowded round it, some of them on their knees on the floor, groping under the cover in an effort to get closer to the dead Sheikh. On the far wall a glass fronted cabinet displayed his *jellabiya,* gown, stick and prayer beads. More people crowded round the cabinet, fingering it reverentially.

Outside a youngish man, with a skullcap perched rakishly low over his forehead, sat on the ground with a gourd filled with what looked like roll–up cigarettes. A group of people surrounded him, pressing pieces of paper and money into his hand.

"This is one of the Sheikh's sons," Amal told me. The pieces of paper accompanied by money were requests for help, she explained, and the rolled–up papers distributed in return, which had verses from the Koran written on them, would bring blessings on the recipient. "Look," she said pointing to a man with a thong tied round his upper arm to which three little leather barrels were attached. "Some people put the bits of paper inside these barrels and wear them all the time. Sometimes they burn the paper or put it in water to soak and then drink the water."

We returned to Sheikh Al Burai's house where Selma and Somaya still sat with Rateb. A group of attendants were serving lunch, carrying in large round trays laid with bowls of mutton soup, a chicken, potato and pumpkin stew, plates of rice and tomato salad.

While we ate I got talking to Rashad, a young American–Sudanese who had come with a group of Sudanese friends. I asked him how he, as an American, viewed the conversion of Westerners to Islam and their interest in living in Sudan.

"I think it comes from an emptiness inside. They're looking for a spiritual life and here in Sudan it's an original place."

"A lot of people from the UK come here," said his friend Yusuf. He went on to tell me the story of six Russian pilots who had wound up in Zariba inadvertently. "Something happened with their plane. It wasn't functioning, it had to land somewhere near here. The Sheikh invited them over. They stayed for fifteen days and then they converted to Islam."

"Most people believe that there's this kind of energy, they feel it with the Sheikh," said Rashad. "I feel it."

Rashad spoke too of the healing powers of the Sheikh. "There are psychiatric patients who come and stay around the house. The way he heals people is by channelling the power of God. He is believed to be closer to God."

Around five o'clock we were taken upstairs to a large alcoved room. The Sheikh lay on the floor on his side in one of the alcoves in a strange kind of position. If I hadn't seen him walking out to his vehicle earlier I would have thought he was paralysed in some way. A *huwar* massaged his feet. We crouched down beside him. "*As salaam aleykum, abuna sheikh.*" A litany of exchanged greetings followed and then the sheikh told us to come back the next morning.

Selma, Somaya and Amal were overjoyed. They had not only met the sheikh, they also had an appointment for a more in–depth talk with him the next day.

The mosque had two guest houses, one for men and one for women. We found the women's.

"Where do we sleep?" Selma asked a young boy who seemed to be in charge.

"There," he said, pointing to a strip of sandy ground.

I must have looked a bit dubious. "We'll give you a *tobe* to lie on," said Somaya.

"No," said Amal. "We'll go to Aisha's house."

So we shouldered our bags, left the religious compound and for the second time that day knocked on Aisha's gate.

"*Ahlan*."

"Can we stay the night here?"

"Of course. *Itfaddalu*."

Darkness was beginning to fall so we dragged the *angaraibs* out into the *hosh* where we would all sleep. I asked for the bathroom. Aisha led me to an area behind one of the round grass huts, picking up a jug of water for me on the way. "There," she pointed. But there was nothing there, no hole in the ground, only several damp patches which, presumably, were the urine of previous visitors. I got on with it.

Back at the *angaraibs* we were now in pitch darkness because Somaya had taken the single oil lamp that Aisha possessed to the shower room. When she came back Aisha accompanied me to take a shower. She attached the lamp to the thatch wall and brought me a bucket of water. I took my clothes off, laid them on the sandy ground, and splashed myself with water from the bucket.

We talked for a while, lying in bed in the dark. Aisha told us she had been betrothed at 11 and had gone to live with her husband at 14. He was a lorry driver and absent for long periods. Whatever the reason – it was not clear – they had separated. Aisha, now 29, earned a meagre living sewing *jellabiyas* and skullcaps which she sold in the market.

When I woke up in the morning Selma, Somaya and Amal were already primped and spruce and ready for their audience with the Sheikh. Selma's blue denim skirt, pink tee shirt and pink chiffon *tarha* of the previous day had been replaced by an impeccable all–black outfit. Somaya had a bottle of body lotion which she was smearing liberally over her legs and passing round to the others. Amal borrowed my Boots skin freshener and marvelled at how shiny it made her face look, not realising that it had merely removed the foundation that she had put on to lighten her own colouring. She put on the black gloves with fake fur trim that she wore to protect her hands from the sun.

Gradually the other members of the family – who had been dispersed to sleep with neighbours to liberate the *angaraibs* for us – drifted back. Aisha's sister milked the goats. Her mother boiled the water for tea over a few lumps of coal burning in a bucket. The two children hovered in the background, fascinated by these sophisticated women from the Gezira and even more so by the *khawaja*.

I wanted to look round the rest of Zariba, and to visit the hospital and *khalwa* that I'd heard about. Selma, Somaya and Amal could go to the Sheikh on their own as they now had an appointment fixed. In any case, I felt a bit of an interloper in the crowd of followers who went to him to get his blessings. I told the women of my plans.

"No, Hilda," said Somaya sternly. "You come with us. If you not come, we not get in. The guard say, where is Hilda? If you not there, he not let us see Sheikh Al Burai."

I couldn't argue with that.

On the way back to the sheikh's house we found him on his way to the Land Rover, surrounded as usual by a swarm of people kissing his hand and pressing messages on to him. There was to be no *majlis* that morning, we were told, Sheikh Al Burai had to go to El Obeid to help sort out some tribal conflict.

I left Selma, Somaya and Amal to fight their way through the mob and started talking with the brother of a man I had seen being brought to the Sheikh's house in a wheelchair the day before. Nasser, the brother, told me that he had suffered brain damage in a car accident two years previously. He was paralysed and had speech and other difficulties. He had been taken to London for treatment to no avail. Now, ready to try anything, the family had brought him to Sheikh Al Burai in the hope that he would be able to cure him.

"Come and meet him," said Nasser.

Mahmoud was sitting on the ground, being spoonfed a ready–mix food by his wife.

"Speak to him," said Nasser. "He can speak English."

"Hello, how are you?"

"Aah faahn."

We spoke a bit more. The words, though barely decipherable showed that he understood what was being said and could respond. He smiled a lot but other than that seemed not to initiate any communication himself. He had already met the Sheikh. There had been no subsequent change in his condition but the family hoped that it might still come about at a later time.

I went back to find that Selma, Somaya and Amal were ecstatic. As well as exchanging the usual greetings with the Sheikh they had somehow managed to tell him about their personal problems and had received some guidance and a blessing. Selma and Somaya were clutching bottles of lemon juice and Amal a bottle of honey, these being commonly given to the Sheikh's followers as gifts.

The three women were taking the truck back to El Obeid. I had decided that, despite the discomfort, I preferred to head straight to Khartoum across the desert in a lorry–bus rather than risk having to spend another night in the $40 hotel.

Contrary to the dire predictions the off–road travel was quite comfortable. The only problem was conditions inside the bus. The seats on the bus were about 12 inches wide and when they were filled more people were crammed in standing. The remaining space was taken up with bags, sacks of grain, goods for the market, live chickens, anything transportable. More people and more goods were packed on to the roof.

A fight broke out between two fat women who were supposed to be in adjoining seats. With one woman seated there was no room for the second. The first one finally ceded her place with martyred mien and the other one sat down. The yelling continued. The hips of the one standing were far wider than the gangway and overflowed into my space, pushing me up against the man to my right. The screaming grew more furious. A black hen at my feet added to the din with a frantic squawking. The bus filled with peals of good–natured laughter from the other passengers.

We stopped in neat villages of thatch and mud. In one of them a group of boys invited me to mount their camel. Gales of laughter sounded from the bus as I pitched forward when the camel raised its hind quarters. More laughter as I lurched in the opposite direction when it rose from its knees. We swayed off for a little walk. The merriment continued as I went through the reverse process to get off again.

Vast tracts of the desert were dotted in regular patterns with the curiously geometrical thorn trees, giving the effect of a formal French garden. Sometimes human figures appeared – a man on a donkey, the coloured flurry of two or three *tobe*s – but with no sign of habitation as far as the eye could see.

There were several toilet stops for the men. They would walk a short distance from the bus and squat down, *jellabiyas* ballooning out around them as they did their business. The ones travelling on the roof had faces like clowns, covered with a thick patina of beige dust. The women stayed on the bus.

Nine and a half hours after leaving Zariba we rolled into the outskirts of Omdurman, driving through a shanty town built out of sacking and cardboard boxes and into the *souk* area, past stacks of foam mattresses, rolls of carpets, stalls piled high with bales of tailoring material, tottering towers of plastic chairs, plastic tables, plastic buckets, pyramids of cooking pots, traffic jammed by donkeys pulling water carts, and ghetto–blaster noise.

I got a taxi from Souk Libya to Khartoum. The top of the windscreen was plastered with an array of photos of religious–looking men, among which I recognised Sheikh Al Burai.

"*Inta sufi?*" I asked the driver. "Are you a Sufi?"

"*Aiwa.* Yes." And he started reeling off the names of all the sheikhs in his portrait gallery.

16 THE CULT OF THE SHEIKH

Back in Khartoum I spoke with Ahmed Babiker, a teacher who is a follower of Sheikh Al Burai. I was puzzled about the cult of the personality fostered so strongly in Zariba, and also with other sheikhs I had come across, which seems so contrary to orthodox Muslim practice.

"Sufis believe you can have someone between you and God to intercede," Ahmed explained, "though Islamic groups don't agree about this. "People believe a sheikh has a special position in his relation with God. Some people are not as clean as others and to have a good relationship with God you must be clean, faithful, a believer, you help others and you love God and you love the Prophet Mohammed very much indeed."

Even stranger was the way in which the sheikh's position was often handed down from generation to generation but Ahmed thought this made sense.

"Those who are clean and faithful and are very close to their fathers are going to be like them. Those who have been chosen by God to be special, their descendants are special also."

The worship of the Sheikh's remains in the tomb also seemed un–Islamic.

"This kind of thing is not advocated," Ahmed agreed, "but at the same time nobody is going to try to stop them."

Another curious thing was the pop song–like quality of the Sheikh's music and the adulation he received for it.

"The Sheikh has been exposed to music in the Sudanese community and this has inspired his style," Ahmed acknowledged. "But his poems and songs mainly praise Prophet Mohammed and promote the good values of Islam. They're full of advice and examples of the life of Prophet Mohammed and his followers at that time. His music inspires you to be with God, it motivates you to repeat the name of God."

As a child Ahmed studied at the *khalwa* at Zariba.

"I was taken to a master who was called a *faki*, meaning someone who is knowledgeable about the whole culture of Islam. In the first stage we were taken to a flat area of ground and we used our fingers to write in the sand, to learn the alphabet. After that we wrote on a slate using local ink made from soot and gum Arabic and a pen made of straw. The teacher used to hold a whip to make the children learn. When it was very, very hot and we were beaten by the teacher I hated it. When things were going well I enjoyed it and we could have fun with our peers. The learning of the Koran was done in chapters and the students sat in a semi circle of six or seven, each one learning a different verse."

Ahmed lived in the *khalwa* with several hundred other boys. "The further you travel the better for you to learn the Koran," he says. "It's better for a child to be away from his family."

Griselda had had experience of Sheikh Al Burai's healing efforts when her husband had a stroke in London.

"While Abdulla was in the Cromwell Hospital in Kensington I got a message that Sheikh Al Burai had summoned Abdulla's family here in Sudan because he was in Khartoum and he wanted them to come to him. One of Abdulla's nieces, Leila, and his sister from El Damer and a whole bunch of them went to Sheikh Al Burai and he gave them a piece of paper on which he had written whatever in his own writing. This was then sent to us in London by DHL. I was quite frankly a bit sceptical about this but Leila my niece was so impressed that she decided it was up to her to carry out the next part of the ritual which meant burning this paper in charcoal in the presence of the sick, paralysed, cerebral haemorrhage–struck Abdulla. On our way from Earl's Court tube station to the hospital Leila came across this Moroccan shop where she was able to buy some kind of charcoal. So we get ourselves into Abdulla's private room in the hospital and then somehow Leila manages to set fire to this charcoal and to burn this holy paper and the next thing is all the fire alarms in the hospital go off and these chaps come dashing in to our room saying: where's the fire, where's the fire? And just that little bit of smoke had set off the whole fire alarm system in that hospital. Then a couple of months later when we finally came back to Sudan and Abdulla was put into the Sahroon hospital in the intensive care unit and Sheikh Al Burai happened to be in town he came to visit him there. I remember there was a great deal of fuss about Sheikh Al Burai coming. And it's quite sure that Sheikh Al Burai has built up a great cult, a personality cult, and he knows how to do it."

Griselda believes, however, that the sheikhs do good work in treating people with psychiatric disorders.

"One of the ways in which they have been very, very useful is that the Sudanese sheikhs, in various places have acted almost as mental hospitals. People who have acute mental problems, the family take them to the sheikh. There are certain sheikhs, all of them away from the towns, where the family of the person stricken with some kind of mental breakdown, schizophrenia, paranoia or whatever would take them. I saw it myself in the 1970s in Abu Gurun. The sheikh had two big compounds, one for men and one for women. We were taken to visit them. One of the ladies who went with me was the wife of the Yugoslav ambassador who was a psychiatrist by profession. The first compound we came to was the men and the second with a separating wall was the women's compound with these little quiet rooms leading off on three sides of this compound and one woman was completely catatonic and then the sheikh came and spoke to her and she was slightly responding to him. Others responded better, and by withdrawing them from the family situation which was the cause of the problem sometimes – like a girl being forced to marry someone she didn't want or a girl who thought she was engaged to a man and then her younger sister came and she got him or whatever – by removing her from this family problem, not only by distance but by actually not being with them and seeing them every day, and then by reading the Koran to them constantly they were often cured by quietism."

But Griselda is scathing about the puffing up of the personalities involved.

"Two years ago I went to the Khartoum flower show, which is an annual show I look forward to, and all these different nurseries, all the people that pride themselves on producing plants, each one had their stand on the ground floor and they were showing the plants that they were proud of and the arrangements that they were proud of, and then there were these competitions for the best rose and the best this and the best that. Then upstairs on the gallery of the Friendship Hall were a number of related things, people who were involved with fertilisers, people who are beekeepers and so on. And at the far end of this gallery there was this enormous display of Korans and prayer mats and there was a big couch, a sort of Madame Recamier couch in gilt with gilded metal and golden satin upholstery. And on the walls were photos of this Dr Hassan Qaribullah, his doctoral certificate from Edinburgh and then a whole framed CV of his life and his works and then there were these famous rosaries called the *elfia* which are made of a thousand nuts from the *nabuq* palm. They are supposed to be used by very religious men because they are very rough and they're not at all polished. You know that there are rosaries in precious stone and in jade and in malachite and in crystal and so on but these are definitely the roughest of the roughest and they're cheap and easy to come by and they're symbolic of poverty and austerity. And then there were one or two, not more than maybe five, ordinary pot plants in ordinary pots. There was a lady there who seemed to be responsible for the place so I just asked her in a rather sarcastic, I must admit, fashion: what is the relevance of all this to the flower show? And she said something about plants are blessed in Islam or in the Koran or something like that, and that's all. And for me it was just a sheer publicity stunt which had got no relevance at all to the flower show. And the following year they were there again."

"When you go to Sheikh Al Burai and when you go to Qaribullah nowadays you find that where there is a concrete house with elaborate courtyards paved in ceramic tiles and where there is a mosque with every latest engineering equipment including loudspeakers and neon lighting the whole poverty thing seems to have got lost and the worldliness is showing its ugly face."

Mikal Mahmoud is sceptical about the whole phenomenon which he sees as comparable to witch doctoring and stemming mainly from African tradition. He is unimpressed by the fact that people go to Zariba and stay there, sometimes for weeks, in grass huts.

"OK, but this is how people live in Sudan. There's no big thing. Yeah, people go there, and they stay there and they eat there and they drink there, and you can go to this other guy near Abu Bakr's house, in Um Bedda in Omdurman. Also people come and they stay there. It's the same thing. Even Qaribullah is known to have people camp out and stay for extended visits. He has facilities to put up people. Even the Sultan down there in Maierno, you find people staying there and doing this. But I want to know, OK, so you went there and you stayed there, what happened? And I never get an answer. There's just an experience of being there.

"You know, Sufism from its roots has nothing to do with this. Sufism from its roots is just that aspect of Islam of cleansing your heart out, moving away from the corporal life for the sake of finding your true self, your inner self or something like this; practising Islam as a refreshed person so that the devil can't tempt you with this life. Sufism evolved as a reaction to the dogmatic Muslims. It's supposed to be a complement to the people that are just into dogma, rules, laws, so that when you put these two things together you have the complete Islam."

17 REFLECTIONS

When I returned to Europe towards the end of 2003 I found that my personal frame of reference had been modified by the experience of five years of life in Sudan.

Searching for my own place in the sun I spent some time in Tuscany. Compared to the spartan simplicity which I had become used to – the rectilinearity, the beigeness of everything – the architecture of Pisa and Lucca and the surrounding medieval villages, and the lush mountainous landscape, seemed to me like a sickeningly rich Black Forest gateau. As a child I had once given up sugar in my tea for Lent. By the time Easter came I could no longer stomach sugary drinks; my palate had been purged of its sweet tooth. Something similar had now happened to my aesthetic sense.

There had also been a shift in perspective in other ways and I often found myself wondering how things would appear to Muslims. An item on the Today programme on Radio 4 on 31 December caught my attention. In anticipation of the New Year's revelry the head barman of the Savoy Hotel had been invited on air to give listeners the recipe for a 'hair of the dog' hangover cure. Amid much laughter and teasing talk about headaches, grogginess and nausea the barman demonstrated the making of a cocktail comprising brandy, crème de menthe and some Italian liqueur which he claimed would have you 'right as rain' in no time. What would teetotal Muslims make of this, I wondered, the idiocy of drinking till you were ill and then trying to cure yourself by drinking even more.

I was bemused at the way in which so many women feel compelled to reveal as much flesh as possible. Almost–naked bodies – women in bikinis, skimpy shorts, sleeveless dresses – looked vulgar and unattractive.

The last time I flew to Khartoum I noticed two women at the airline check–in. One was British. She wore a sleeveless orange tee shirt revealing grubby bra straps. A roll of fat bulged through the 2–inch gap between tee shirt and jeans. The jeans had a slashed tear just under the left buttock. Beside her was a Muslim woman in a beige ankle–length robe. Her head was swathed Tuareg–like in a beige floral covering. Both aesthetically and in terms of sexual appeal she beat the British woman hands down. I could imagine that being shrouded in veils might heighten a woman's awareness of her own sexuality, the very hiding of herself reminding her constantly of her potential attractiveness to men. The British wife of a Sudanese, had said as much to me in talking of her feelings about wearing the *hijab* during the *umra*. "I had to wear the *hijab* from the time I left the house in Khartoum. It was lovely. I love the idea of hiding yourself just for your husband."

Jane Anne reported noticing similar shifts in some of the oil company families that came to her riding school.

"Even the Canadians that came, Talisman, they said before they went away, and even the kids said, that they felt nicer wearing long tee shirts and trousers. The teenage girls, they said they felt much safer here in Sudan, and the boys weren't glaring at them and thinking: hm, hm, hm, there's a girl, and things like that. And they said that they thought they would find it very difficult to go back to the way they were. In fact, I had a couple of emails from some of the girls that went back with the Talisman lot and they said it was very difficult for the first year to actually get back into the way of being in Canada."

Critical comments about the way people dress in the West were common among foreigners who had spent some time in Sudan, and also about bad language and inappropriate sexual behaviour. Before Deirdre went to Sudan she was warned that there should be no public displays of affection. "I found this very restricting and felt spontaneity had gone out of one's relationship," she says. "But now I cringe when I see couples in England in intimate embraces."

While these changes were being wrought in the perspectives of foreigners living in the country, Sudan itself had been undergoing its own changes.

During the fifteen years of the Bashir government the social and religious climate had moved from one of severe repression in the 1990s in the direction of a more relaxed one in the latter few years.

The Public Order Act of 1991, part of the regime's new penal code, had impinged with renewed severity on just about all areas of Sudanese life. Greater restrictions were placed on social gatherings to prevent the mixing of males and females. Women in particular were subject to harassment. Any woman accompanied in public by a man not related to her, any woman seen to be waiting 'too long' for a bus, risked being arrested on suspicion of immorality. The Islamic dress code was rigidly enforced and an attempt – unsuccessful – was even made to replace the Sudanese *tobe* with an Iranian–style *chador*. A ban was imposed on unaccompanied women travelling abroad. A 1994 ruling clamped down on wedding parties, decreeing that they must end before sunset prayers and be supervised by sheikhs and the police. A 1998 law imposed the segregation of the sexes on public transport. Another law banned women from dancing in the presence of men.

Shortly after I arrived in 1999 a group of female students were flogged in public for being improperly dressed at a riverside picnic. At that time the Public Order police maintained a high profile. No Muslim woman would dare to be seen outside with her head uncovered.

Four years later female headgear was becoming increasingly daring. The *tarha*, which was intended to reduce women's attractiveness to men, was becoming more of a fashion statement, both in design and the way it was being worn. It was quite common to see women with their hair tied back in a knot and the *tarha* suspended from the knot, or merely tossed round the neck, ready to be hitched up if necessary. Figure–hugging skirts which would have had the wearer hauled into a police truck a few years previously were becoming the norm.

In the mid 90s the government supported a campaign to outlaw all secular music. In 1994 a professional violinist was beaten up by security police who smashed his violin and told him he should stop playing music and turn to Islam. In the same year a fanatic, fired by the belief that music is an abomination, stabbed to death a singer at the Musician's Club. The Sudanese superstar singer and human rights activist Mohammed Wardi could sing only in exile.

In October 2003 a cultural show was held at Friendship Hall in Khartoum, the first event of its kind for twelve years. Groups of men and women appeared on the stage together, performing the tribal dances of Sudan with their pounding rhythms and suggestive movements. The heads of the women were uncovered. Former president Nimeiri was there with the Minister of Culture and a number of prominent academics. One of the singers was Mohammed Wardi.

Three years previously a young Mexican missionary I knew was abducted and tortured by the security police. He was so traumatised by the experience that he had to leave the country. Sudan at the time was being described by the U.S. State Department's Office of International Religious Freedom as suffering "the worst religious persecution in the world".

In October 2003, in anticipation of the expected peace, *Sudan Vision*, an English–language daily, announced the start of Sunday Vision, a weekly double page "dedicated to Christians in Sudan". During a return visit to Sudan in March 2004 I attended a showing of Mel Gibson's controversial film *The Passion* in the house of a Christian in Khartoum. She had invited about twenty–five guests, both Muslim and Christian. After the film an American pastor hosted a discussion about the life and death of Christ and what he represented for the two religions. Both Muslims and Christians contributed in a spirit of goodwill, agreeing on areas of common ground and being relaxed about their dogmatic differences.

For social occasions foreign embassies in Khartoum provide two bars: one serving alcohol to cater for non–Muslim guests and one with soft drinks only. During the 1990s no Sudanese Muslim would dare be seen going to the alcohol bar. At most, he might surreptitiously ask a foreign friend to get him something. In recent years, many Muslim guests have been losing their inhibitions about drinking openly on these occasions.

Towards the end of 2003 the Sahafa newspaper was closed down for three days as a punishment for running an advertisement for holidays in Paris which included a reference to the good wine that can be found there. But the incident incited no anger, only ridicule. There was the feeling that the days when the government could get away with this kind of thing were coming to an end.

The political developments were reflected in the changing commercial face of Khartoum. The sight of peace on the horizon, coupled with the recently started flow of petrodollars, was giving entrepreneurs the confidence to invest in upgrading their services and facilities. New office blocks were going up, shops were being refurbished, a rash of smart private clinics appeared, more Internet cafés, more pizza restaurants, more burger bars. A shopping mall, à la Singapore, opened in March 2004. Nothing of the like had ever been seen in Sudan. It houses a bowling alley, a cinema, restaurants and a large supermarket; shops such as Homes R Us, Toys R Us, and clothing retailers selling Pierre Cardin, U2 and Mango. A Gaudiesque structure shades a recreational area outside.

The whole environment was beginning to take on a different look. An army of workers in turquoise and yellow jumpsuits with matching hats and turquoise and yellow refuse trucks was now deployed to keep the city clean. Even the tea ladies were smartening up their "premises", keeping the area round their braziers carefully swept and bounded by neat little semi circles of stones for customers to sit on. Miraculously, name plates appeared on the previously anonymous streets. Everybody seemed to be chattering into a mobile phone.

Yet in some ways it seemed to be two steps forward and two steps back.

As the conflict between north and south eased towards a resolution, the conflict in the Darfur region in the west worsened. In February 2003 fighting had broken out between groups of ethnic Africans and militia groups from neighbouring Arabised tribes. Over the next year the Arab militias, with the support of government forces, pursued a campaign of ethnic cleansing against non–Arab civilians who were being bombed, massacred, maimed and driven from their homes.

At the same time as *Sudan Vision* was opening up its pages to the Christians of Sudan the *Khartoum Monitor,* an English–language daily serving the city's southern population, was being subjected to repeated shutdowns by the government and its managing editor forced to flee the country.

Controversial *sharia* judgements were still being made. In December 2003 a 16–year–old single mother was sentenced to a public flogging of 100 lashes in Kalakla. Her claim that she had been raised as a Christian and was therefore not eligible for this type of punishment was ignored by the judge. In March 2004 a farmer in Darfur was sentenced to cross–amputation in a trial in which no defence was allowed.

Jane Anne had spoken of the culture of caring fostered in Sudan by the way children are brought up.

"In England you feed a baby, you change it, you put it to bed. If it cries for twenty minutes, it cries for twenty minutes. Here it's so totally different. If Zeinab goes *eeee* everyone's saying, oh what's the matter. In England they're in their cots most of the day. Here they don't get put in cots. They're with somebody being cuddled and loved the whole day long. So this grows up in them, the love and affection towards other people. I really do like that about Sudan."

At the time she was speaking three out of four children deposited in the government–run Mygoma orphanage were dying due to inadequate nutrition, poor hygiene and lack of medical care. Mygoma accommodates abandoned newborn babies, mostly born to single Muslim women who would incur terrible retribution if their pregnancies were discovered. Of the 516 taken in in the year 2000, 433 died. When Médecins Sans Frontières became involved in 2003 they reported finding a 75 per cent mortality rate. A British woman who worked there as a volunteer told me of a healthy 2–day old baby who was handed in by its mother, a university student. A week later it was dead of neglect. As the director had said to Griselda's friend: you can take him if you like because they're only going to die in here.

At the same time thousands of street children, mostly from the displaced population, roamed the streets of Khartoum, the luckier ones working – shining shoes, selling plastic bags, doing domestic chores – the others begging and stealing to stay alive.

All the converts praised Sudan as a very safe place to live. They felt that they and their families were better protected from both physical and moral harm there than in Europe or America.

Yet for years human rights groups have been signalling abuses and atrocities perpetrated in Sudan. Reference to Amnesty International, Human Rights Watch, Vigilance Sudan and many more reveals a catalogue of cruelty facilitated by war and fired by religious intolerance and racism: widespread raping and looting by soldiers, dragooning of child soldiers in both north and south, demolition of churches and housing in the shanty towns, routine torture and ill–treatment in the so–called "ghost houses" where people were detained incommunicado without charge or trial.

When I started this book I was working on a writing assignment for UNICEF. One of my stories focused on the issue of abduction. Sudan has a long history of slave–raiding which continues till today, with one Arab tribe in particular, the cattle–herding Baggara, preying on African tribes to the south. I interviewed two children who had been rescued from their captors.

13–year–old Acuen was living with his mother in a hut made of cardboard cartons on the banks of the Nile in Khartoum.

Five years previously a band of militiamen attacked his village in Bahr el Gazal in Southern Sudan, burning the houses and forcing the inhabitants to flee to the forest. Acuen, his mother and his younger brother, aged 2, were captured by the attackers and borne off to different destinations.

For the next two years Acuen worked as a cowherd, tending the cattle of a nomadic family. His mother, Nyibol, was put to work for another family, cooking and fetching water and firewood. Neither knew where the other was, nor did they know what had happened to the younger child.

After nine months Nyibol managed to escape. With the help of a Dinka retrieval team she started to look for her children. After five months Acuen was tracked down and released. His little brother had still not been found.

10–year–old Akundo was snatched up by a man on horseback in identical circumstances to Acuen's at the age of 5. When she was rescued two years later she had forgotten both her name and her tribal language.

The retrieval team had reunited Akundo with an uncle's family. They had no home of their own but lived temporarily as caretakers on the site of a house under construction. We crouched amid a welter of rubble, trailing cables, oil drums and squawking hens as we talked through a Dinka interpreter. Akundo's arms moved in a repetitive up and down motion like those of a string puppet as she described her life as a goatherd with a family who regularly beat her. Her uncle had no news of her parents and no means of contacting them in the SPLA–held territory where they lived.

I later ran some workshops with a group of displaced teachers from the South to work on a series of children's stories on the theme of peace and reconciliation in Sudan. Our brainstorming elicited graphic confirmation of the stories more soberly expressed in the aid agency reports. They too spoke of abducted children and their concern that many of them were sent to *khalwas* by their masters and forcibly converted to Islam; also of abducted women being raped or forced into marriage with their captors.

Selma, the chairperson of a teachers' association which I was helping, turned up for a meeting one day in late 2003 devastated by news she had just received. Her family village in the west of Sudan had been bombed to smithereens by government planes. She had no idea what had happened to her relatives, whether they had been killed, raped or abducted like so many already, or whether they had taken flight with the hundreds of thousands of displaced persons dispersed into the open countryside, struggling to stay alive, or swarming over the border into Chad. By mid–2004 the conflict had escalated to a point where the United Nations was describing it as "the world's worst humanitarian crisis". There were reports of Janjaweed militiamen indulging in the mass rape of women and young girls from the African tribes and breaking their arms and legs to prevent them escaping; of women from the Arab tribes watching and singing for joy; and of Darfur villagers being chained together and burned alive. Aid organisations were predicting disease, starvation and death on a massive scale, all of it man–made.

These stories all conjure up a world which is the antithesis of the one described by the converts. They tell of the kinds of social evil – child neglect, rape, kidnapping, beatings – which the converts claim to be sheltered from in Sudan, and they tell also of far worse outrages.

But none of these stories negate or diminish the truth of what the converts have said. It's just that their truth is only one of many different truths about Sudan.

Sudan is as if made up of disparate communities and what the converts report is true for the community to which they belong. Much of it is also true for the wider community as, despite the traumas and abuses, the murder and the mayhem, the neighbourliness and community spirit are still largely preserved.

One of the conundrums of Sudan is how to reconcile the relaxed demeanour and the unfailing good nature of most of the people with the terrible goings–on.

For Deirdre the answer lies in the inherent fatalism of the Sudanese, the belief that whatever happens is the will of God. "It's God's will if things go wrong and so you must accept it. As individuals they can be absolutely charming. They are basically hospitable, generous and fatalistic and nothing seems to faze them."

Another puzzle is how people can move to a country where so many atrocities are perpetrated. But it is the charm, hospitality and generosity mentioned by Deirdre that are to the fore in the communities inhabited by the converts, as it was for Deirdre and me. This is not only part of the fabric of their daily lives, it is also a cocoon against what is happening beyond.

18 LOOKING FORWARD

Early in 2004, the peace negotiations between the government and the Sudan People's Liberation Army of the South were coming closer to a conclusion. One of the final sticking points was *sharia* law. Southerners could not agree to being subject to the laws of a religion which was not theirs. The Government of Sudan could not agree to abolishing *sharia* for the Muslim north because to do so would be acting against Islam. A compromise was sought: *sharia* in the north and secular law in the south. But this left the problem of Khartoum, which would be the capital for the whole country. The two sides wrangled for weeks over a proposal that Khartoum, or part of it, should be declared a *sharia*–free zone.

Griselda saw this as a crystallisation of the power struggle between north and south.

"This is the last battle between the so–called Christian/Pagan south and the Muslim north. And quite honestly I cannot see that you could have freedom of drinking and whatever you like in the capital and not have it somewhere else because it would be like America during Prohibition. There would be smuggling between one area and the other. I personally think it would be better to leave the whole country free to do what they like because it worked very well before."

But *sharia* is far easier to impose than to repeal. Any Muslim politician revoking *sharia* could be accused of apostasy, a crime punishable by death under Islamic law.

The problem is not that *sharia* can't be abolished, Griselda says, but that nobody wants to take responsibility for it. "Nobody dares to be the one that abolishes it because the next thing is

Osama Bin Laden will send someone to assassinate him."

. Abdel Karim thought that the abolition of *sharia* could lead to society deteriorating to the extent that he might no longer feel able to stay in Sudan.

"I feel that if *sharia* disappears then there's going to be terrible disruptions to the happiness and the security and the tranquillity that people have enjoyed in this country. I'm concerned that people are going to be really quite keen in this new age of peace to do things they never did before. So you're going to see a lot more confrontations. For example, the majority of people in Sudan don't find it acceptable that people are drinking in the street, don't find it acceptable that women are dressed in lurid kinds of ways. All of this will create a more heightened Islamic extremism. And at the same time you will find that pockets of society will become crime pockets. Because of all this influx of anti–Islamic practices you are going to be subject to the same situation you find in any of the other African cities around the country and in any of the European capitals of the world. And that is insecurity, crime, things that have been minimised in Sudan. If this happens I will live in the country. If it reaches me in the country I will leave. I've always been concerned to live my life as best as I can. That's why I came here. So if I'm not able to do that, if the environment has been disturbed by people who really don't respect themselves or others, then I will find somewhere else where the environment is slightly better for me."

In the event, when a peace agreement was signed in May 2004, *sharia* was retained for the whole of Northern Sudan including Khartoum, but with non–Muslims being exempt from it. It was agreed that a separate system consistent with the local faiths would be applied in the south.

Despite the retention of *sharia*, the need to cater for the different lifestyles of non–Muslims and increased dealings with the West will undoubtedly push towards a further easing of restrictions and a greater permissiveness. Will this Sudan still be an environment in which Western converts will feel at ease or will they, like the

American teachers at the BEI school, want to go back home or move on somewhere else?

Lena already sees a lot of Western influences coming in, especially among the better off, but feels that she has more freedom here to live in the way she chooses.

"In America you feel constrained. Society's like a rat race, the government's always on your head, over your shoulder. Here you can practise as a Muslim freely, without being afraid that some racist is going to harass you or maybe you'll get shot down or maybe the police will discriminate against you or question you just because you're a Muslim, because after September 11 they were hauling in all kinds of people just because they were Muslim."

Naimah is resigned to things being less than ideal and thinks that even with the expected changes she and her family will still be happy to stay in Sudan. Regarding the unofficial relaxation of the dress code which already enables women to pay little more than lip service to the idea of covering their heads, she says: "When I saw that I said, well, it's better than seeing naked butts and boobs. You have to take the lesser of the evils."

Abdel Karim fears that a peace negotiated between the government and the SPLA will be followed by conflicts of another kind unless efforts are made to bring people together and settle unresolved grievances.

"I'm concerned that peace in this country without reconciliation is going to cause more friction and more problems. Without reconciliation as we've seen perhaps like in South Africa there's still going to be resentment and bitterness especially among the Southerners who have been poorly treated. So therefore my concern, unless there is true reconciliation whereby people are saying sorry – and I've not heard this said yet – enmity that exists between people will flare up as we've seen in Nigeria where the enmity between Christians and Muslims has led to running battles in streets, thousands of people dying and being killed for religious clashes."

For Mikal the question is not so important as he plans to leave Khartoum and take his family to his wife's home town of Kassala where he has already bought some land. But in any case he doesn't think improved economic conditions or increased Western influence will have much impact on the Sudanese.

"Since I've been in Sudan there's been quite a lot of development in the infrastructure and the economy. Things are now available in the market, people are into the Internet, everybody has a mobile phone. But I don't think that this is bringing about much of a change in the hearts of the people. They're still Sudanese and that I don't think is ever going to go away. Money doesn't change them and going to America doesn't change them, and I don't think it's going to change them in the near future although maybe after twenty years, thirty years we might see a different Sudan. Being Sudanese is not something related to the *sharia* or even to Islam."

For Mohammed Abdul Qaadir, Naimah and Khalid too there will be little change. No matter what happens in Khartoum it is unlikely to affect them in the villages where they intend to settle.

Jane Anne has no doubt at all about where she wants to live.

"I can honestly say even if, God forbid, Yazin died, or we got divorced or we split up or something I would definitely stay here, I wouldn't go back to live in England."

For the others too, there will be No Going Back.

GLOSSARY OF TERMS

Abreh – Drink made from sorghum

Alhamdulillah – Thanks be to God

Angaraib – Rope bed used for both sitting and sleeping

Aragi – Date–based alcoholic drink

Asida – Porridge made from sorghum or maize

Baraka – Special spiritual power, state of blessedness

Bika – Funeral

Da'awah – Invitation to Islam

Dakhlia – Student hostel

Dua' – Supplication

Dukhan – Smoke bath for beautifying the skin

Fiqh – Islamic jurisprudence

Ful – Egyptian beans, dish made with these beans

Faki – Muslim holy man

Hadith – The speech and acts of Prophet Mohammed

Halal – Approved by Islamic law

Haram – Forbidden by Islamic law

Hijab – Islamic head covering

Hijra – Migration from a non–Muslim to a Muslim land; originally hegira, the flight of Mohammed from Mecca to Medina to escape persecution

Hosh – Enclosed yard of Sudanese house

Hudud – Punishments prescribed by Islamic law

Huwar – Follower of a Sufi order

Inshallah – God willing

Jama'a – Community

Jellabiya – Long white robe worn by Northern Sudanese men

Jinn – Type of spirit

Karkade – Drink made from hibiscus leaves

Khalwa – Islamic school, mainly for the study of the Koran

Khawaja – Foreigner, usually a white foreigner

Muhajiroun – People who make hijra

Mulah – Stew

Masjid – Mosque

Najassa – Dirty, especially in relation to worship

Niqab – Islamic face covering

Rakuba – Straw shelter, usually with open sides

Salat – Prayers

Shahada – Muslim profession of faith, recited when converting
to Islam

Sharia – Islamic law, governing both religious and secular life

Sheesha – Arab water pipe

Shia – The smaller of the two main branches of Islam

Sheikha – Leader of a zar ceremony

Sunna – The area of Muslim law based on Prophet Mohammed's
words or acts

Sunni – The larger of the two main branches of Islam

Sura – Chapter of the Koran

Tamia – Ground chickpea balls

Tarha – Scarf worn over the head

Tasawwuf – Sufism

Tobe – Over garment worn by Northern Sudanese women consisting of a long strip of material wound loosely round the body and over the head

Tariqa – Sufi sect

Umra – Minor pilgrimage to Mecca

Wahhabi – Strictly orthodox Sunni Muslim sect, predominant in Saudi Arabia

Wudu – Ritual washing before prayer

Yom as samaya – Baby's naming day

Zar – Spirit cult involving possession and healing

Zikr – Sufi worshipping ritual

Coming Soon

My Journey With A Remarkable Tree - Ken Finn

1903070384, £9.99, Travel Writing and Natural History

Ken Finn set out exploring Cambodia to indulge his passion and fascination with trees. What he found was certainly moving but in a much bleaker way than he had ever imagined; systematic, cheap, and thoughtless destruction of ancient forests for pathetic and immediate economic gratification. The effect was to fire in him an unexpected anger, which became the fuel for a determination to discover what was really going on. His journey became a mission as he followed his once remarkable tree on its miserable way from spirit forest to the furniture corner of a home-counties garden centre.

Discovery Road - Tim Garrett and Andy Brown

0953057534, £9.99, Travel Writing

Follow Tim and Andy as they leave behind the daily grind of everyday life and become first people to mountain bike unsupported around the world, traversing the vast deserts of Australia, the dangerous bushlands of Africa and the awesome Andes Mountain range of South America. It is a fast moving, inspirational tale of self-discovery: full of adventure, conflict, humour, danger and a multitude of colourful characters. Much more than a travelogue, it proves that ordinary people can chase great dreams.

Zohra's Ladder - Pamela Windo

1903070406, £9.99, Travel Writing

Zohra's Ladder is a wondrous collection of stories of Moroccan life that offer a privileged immersion into a world of deep sensuality. Pamela Windo chronicles her unexpected love affair with the country and its people, peeling back layers of history, of paint, of finely embroidered fabric to find the truths in the mysterious and the exotic. Her stories are of snatched affairs, unforeseen warmth, subtle eroticism in shadowed courtyards. The result are liberating and uplifting portraits of the places and people she finds told with an extraordinary delicacy.

Blood, Sweat and Charity - Nick Stanhope
1903070414, £9.99,Travel Guide

Blood, Sweat and Charity is the most practical guide to self-help and empowerment you will ever read. It is about giving you the tools to fulfil that extraordinary dream, whatever it might be, that transforms the rest of your life. The book explains not just why but how you might want to set your life-changing challenge; from plotting the route to deciding who to take with you and everything in between. Written by someone with the saddle sores and psychological scars to know how it feels, Blood Sweat and Charity is about how to really make a difference to yourself and to the world.

Death - Herbie Brennan
1903070422, £9.99, History

Death is about exactly what it says it is about: the multitudinous ways to end human life. Brennan explores the great plagues of history, the epic human destruction caused by war, nature's mass killers, and every other means of expiration as a prelude to discussing what comes next. He draws on ancient texts, science, religion, folklore, literature, dismantling taboo in a quest for meanings. A compulsive study, its effect is strangely liberating and life-enhancing.

The Accidental Optimists Guide to Life - Emily Joy
1903070430, £9.99, Non-fiction Chic Lit

The Accidental Optimist's Guide to Life explores Emily's inimitable philosophy of hope and humour through the example of her own ups and downs. It tells the story of optimism triumphing what might elsewhere be the makings of disappointment, despair, exhaustion or just low-level irritation; births, illnesses, family deaths, and problem pets. It is a classic in the genre of generating remarkable insights out of living through the seemingly unremarkable. And it is funny.

Changing The World: Step by Step - Michael Meegan

1903070449, £9.99, Mind, Body, Spirit

Many people say they want to make a difference in the world. But they don't know how. Changing the world, step by step offers examples of how real people have made real differences on all levels, global, local and personal. It reminds us to see the joy and love in every moment of every day. And that making a difference is something everyone can do. You can start changing the world simply by buying this book. The profits will go directly to help AIDS orphans in Africa. Your first step in making a difference.

100 Ways to Change The World - Michael Meegan

1903070457, £4.99, Mind, Body, Spirit and Self Help

Many people want to make a difference in the world but are unsure how to. 100 Ways To Change the World does what it says and gives examples of how we can make a difference. By smiling at a stranger or helping someone across the road, it reminds us to see the joy and love in every moment of every day and that making a difference is something everyone can do. The perfect companion to Changing The World Step by Step.

AUDIO CD

Green Oranges on Lion Mountain - Emily Joy

1903070465, £9.99, Travel - Audio CD

Emily Joy puts on her rose-tinted specs, leaves behind her comfortable life as a GP in York and heads off for two years to a remote hospital in Sierra Leone. There she finds the oranges are green, the bananas are black and her patients are, well, really ill. There's no water, no electricity, no oxygen, no amputation saw and Dr. Em is no surgeon. And there's no chocolate to treat her nasty case of unrequited love. Then the rebels invade

Recent Titles

Riding the Outlaw Trail - Simon Casson
A true story of an epic horseback journey by two Englishmen from
Mexico to Canada, across 2,000 miles of some of America's most
difficult terrain. Their objective? To retrace the footsteps of those
legendary real life bandits Butch Cassidy and the Sundance Kid, by
riding the outlaw trails they rode more than a century ago.
ISBN: 1 903070 228. Price £9.99.

Desert Governess - Phyllis Ellis
Phyllis, a former Benny Hill actress, takes on a new challenge when
she becomes a governess to the Saudi Arabian Royal family. In this
frank personal memoir, she gives us an insider's view into the Royal
family and a woman's role in this mysterious kingdom.
ISBN: 1 903070 015. Price £9.99.

Last of the Nomads - W. J. Peasley
Warri and Yatungka were the last of the desert nomads to live
permanently in the traditional way. Their deaths marked the end
of a tribal lifestyle that stretched back more than 30,000 years. The
Last of the Nomads tells of an extraordinary journey in search of
Warri and Yatungka, their rescue and how they survived alone for
thirty years in the unrelenting Western Desert region of Australia.
ISBN: 1 903070 325. Price £9.99.

All Will Be Well - Michael Meegan
So many self help books look internally to provide inspiration,
however this book looks at how love and compassion when given
out to others, can act as a better antidote to the human condition
than trying to inwardly solve feelings of discontentment.
ISBN: 1 903070 279. Price £9.99.

First Contact - Mark Anstice

This is a true story of a modern day exploration by two young adventurers and the discovery of cannibal tribes in the 21st century. An expedition far more extraordinary than they had ever imagined, one that would stretch them, their friendship and their equipment to the limits.

ISBN: 1 903070 260. Price £9.99.

Further Travellers' Tales From Heaven and Hell - Various

This is the third book in the series, after the first two best selling Travellers' Tales from Heaven and Hell. It is an eclectic collection of over a hundred anecdotal travel stories which will enchant you, shock you and leave you in fits of laughter!

ISBN: 1 903070 112. Price £9.99.

Special Offa - Bob Bibby

Following his last best selling book Dancing with Sabrina, Bob walks the length of Offa's Dyke. He takes us through the towns and villages that have sprung up close by and reveals their ancient secrets and folklore. He samples the modern day with his refreshingly simple needs and throws light on where to go and what to see.

ISBN: 1 903070 287. Price £9.99.

Baghdad Business School - Heyrick Bond Gunning

A camp bed, ten cans of baked beans, some water and $25,000 is all that was needed to set up an International Business in Iraq. The book chronicles an amusing description of the trials and tribulations of doing business in an environment where explosions and shootings are part of everyday life, giving the reader a unique insight into what is really happening in this country.

ISBN: 1 903070 333. Price £9.99.

The Good Life - Dorian Amos
Needing a change and some adventure, Dorian and his wife
searched their world atlas and decided to sell up and move to
Canada. Having bought Pricey the car, Boris Lock their faithful dog,
a canoe and their fishing equipment they set off into the Yukon
Wilderness to find a place they could call home.
ISBN: 1 903070 309. Price £9.99.

Green Oranges on Lion Mountain - Emily Joy
Armed with a beginner's guide to surgery, GP Emily Joy took up
her VSO posting at a remote hospital in Sierra Leone. As she set off
into the unknown, action, adventure and romance were high on
her agenda; rebel forces and the threat of civil war were not.
ISBN: 1 903070 295. Price £9.99.

The Con Artist Handbook - Joel Levy
Get wise with The Con Artist's Handbook as it blows the lid on the
secrets of the successful con artist and his con games. Get inside
the hustler's head and find out what makes him tick; Learn how the
world's most infamous scams are set up and performed; Peruse the
career profiles of the most notorious scammers and hustlers of all time;
Learn to avoid the modern-day cons of the e-mail and Internet age.
ISBN: 1 903070 341. Price £9.99.

The Forensics Handbook - Pete Moore
The Forensic Handbook is the most up-to-date log of forensic
techniques available. Discover how the crime scene is examined
using examples of some of the most baffling crimes; Learn
techniques of lifting and identifying prints; Calculate how to
examine blood splatter patterns; Know what to look for when
examining explosive deposits, especially when terrorist activity is
suspected. Learn how the Internet is used to trace stalkers.
ISBN: 1 903070 35X. Price £9.99.

Lost Lands Forgotten Stories - Alexandra Pratt
Inspired by Mina Hubbard who made an astonishing 600 mile river
journey in 1905 to restore the reputation of her late husband who
had died on the same route, Alexandra Pratt retraces Hubbard's
steps through the wild and ancient land of Labrador as she
confronts an unforgiving landscape that surprises her at every turn.

ISBN: 1 903070 368. Price £9.99

Also by Eye Books

Jasmine and Arnica - Nicola Naylor
A blind woman's journey around India.
ISBN: 1 903070 171. Price £9.99.

Touching Tibet - Niema Ash
A journey into the heart of this intriguing forbidden kingdom.
ISBN: 1 903070 18X. Price £9.99.

Behind the Veil - Lydia Laube
A shocking account of a nurses Arabian nightmare.
ISBN: 1 903070 198. Price £9.99.

Walking Away - Charlotte Metcalf
A well known film makers African journal.
ISBN: 1 903070 201. Price £9.99.

Travels in Outback Australia - Andrew Stevenson
In search of the original Australians - the Aboriginal People.
ISBN: 1 903070 147. Price £9.99

The European Job - Jonathan Booth
10,000 miles around Europe in a 25 year old classic car.
ISBN: 1 903070 252. Price £9.99

Around the World with 1000 Birds - Russell Boyman
An extraordinary answer to a mid-life crisis.
ISBN: 1 903070 163. Price £9.99

Cry from the Highest Mountain - Tess Burrows
A climb to the point furthest from the centre of the earth.
ISBN: 1 903070 120. Price £9.99

Dancing with Sabrina - Bob Bibby
A journey from source to sea of the River Severn.
ISBN: 1 903070 244. Price £9.99

Grey Paes and Bacon - Bob Bibby
A journey around the canals of the Black Country
ISBN: 1 903070 066. Price £7.99

Jungle Janes - Peter Burden
Twelve middle-aged women take on the Jungle. As seen on Ch 4.
ISBN: 1 903070 05 8. Price £7.99

Travels with my Daughter - Niema Ash
Forget convention, follow your instincts.
ISBN: 1 903070 04 X. Price £7.99

Riding with Ghosts - Gwen Maka
One woman's solo cycle ride from Seattle to Mexico.
ISBN: 1 903070 00 7. Price £7.99

Riding with Ghosts: South of the Border - Gwen Maka
The second part of Gwen's epic cycle trip across the Americas.
ISBN: 1 903070 09 0. Price £7.99

Triumph Round the World - Robbie Marshall
He gave up his world for the freedom of the road.
ISBN: 1 903070 08 2. Price £7.99

Fever Trees of Borneo - Mark Eveleigh
A daring expedition through uncharted jungle.
ISBN: 0 953057 56 9. Price £7.99

Frigid Women - Sue and Victoria Riches
The first all-female expedition to the North Pole.
ISBN: 0 953057 52 6. Price £7.99

Jungle Beat - Roy Follows
Fighting Terrorists in Malaya.
ISBN: 0 953057 57 7. Price £7.99

Slow Winter - Alex Hickman
A personal quest against the backdrop of the war-torn Balkans.
ISBN: 0 953057 58 5. Price £7.99

Tea for Two - Polly Benge
She cycled around India to test her love.
ISBN: 0 953057 59 3. Price £7.99

Traveller's Tales from Heaven and Hell - Various
A collection of short stories from a nationwide competition.
ISBN: 0 953057 51 8. Price £6.99

More Traveller's Tales from Heaven and Hell - Various
The second collection of short stories.
ISBN: 1 903070 02 3. Price £6.99

A Trail of Visions: Route 1 - Vicki Couchman
A stunning photographic essay.
ISBN: 1 871349 338. Price £14.99

A Trail of Visions: Route 2 - Vicki Couchman
The second stunning photographic essay.
ISBN: 0 953057 50 X. Price £16.99

Book Microsites

If you are interested in finding out more about this book please visit our book microsite:

www.eye-books.com/seekingsanctuary/home.htm

We have also created microsites for a number of our other new books including:

Riding The Outlaw Trail
Desert Governess
The Last of the Nomads
First Contact
Special Offa
The Good Life
Green Oranges on Lion Mountain
Baghdad Business School
Lost Lands Forgotten Stories

For details on these sites and others which we are developing please visit our main website:

www.eye-books.com

Special Offers and Promotions

We are offering our club members and people who have read this book the opportunity to take advantage of promotions on our other books by buying direct from us.

For information on these special offers please visit the following page of our website:

www.eye-books.com/promotions.htm

About Eye Books

Eye books is a young, dynamic publishing company that likes to break the rules. Our independence allows us to publish books which challenge the way people see things. It also means that we can offer new authors a platform from which they can shine their light and encourage others to do the same.

To date we have published 50 books that cover a number of genres including Travel, Biography, Adventure and History. Many of our books are experience driven. All of them are inspirational and life-affirming.

Frigid Women, for example, tells the story of the world-record making first all female expedition to the North Pole. A fifty year-old mother of three who had recently recovered from a mastectomy, and her daughter are the authors neither had ever written a book before. Sue Riches is now both author and highly sought after motivational speaker.

We also publish thematic anthologies, such as The Tales from Heaven and Hell series, for those who prefer the short story format. Here everyone has the chance to get their stories published and win prizes such as flights to any destination in the world.

And here's what makes us really different: As well as publishing books, Eye Books has set up a club for like-minded people and is in the process of developing a number of initiatives and services for its community of members. After all, the more you put into life, the more you get out of it.

Please visit www.eye-books.com for further information.

Eye Club Membership

Each month, we receive hundreds of enquiries' from people who have read our books, discovered our website or entered our competitions. All of these people have certain things in common; a desire to achieve, to extend the boundaries of everyday life and to learn from others' experiences.

Eye Books has, therefore, set up a club to unite these like-minded people. It is a community where members can exchange ideas, contact authors, discuss travel, both future and past as well as receive information and offers from ourselves.

Membership is free.

Benefits of the Eye Club

As a member of the Eye Club:

• You are offered the invaluable opportunity to contact our authors directly.
• You will be able to receive a regular newsletter, information on new book releases and company developments as well as discounts on new and past titles.
• You can attend special member events such as book launches, author talks and signings.
• Receive discounts on a variety of travel related products and services from Eye Books partners.
• In addition, you can enjoy entry into Eye Books competitions including the ever popular Heaven and Hell series and our monthly book competition.

To register your membership, simply visit our website and register on our club pages: www.eye-books.com.